VILLAGE PEOPLE
SKETCHES OF AUBURN

Essays by
John M. Williams

Solomon & George Publishers
108 South 8th Street
Opelika, AL 36801

1. Auburn, Alabama. 2. Essays. 3. Memoir.

ISBN: 978-0-9966839-5-1

First Edition
10 9 8 7 6 5 4 3 2 1

Cover Design by Iris Saya Miller

Front cover photo of the Sani-Freeze is courtesy of Auburn University Library Special Collections and Archives Department. Other photos used on the cover are acknowledged where they are found within the book.

TABLE OF CONTENTS

Foreword

When the light is right, you can look at my friend Johnny Williams and see Lord Byron. That is, a Lord Byron without the weight problem or club foot, but a handsome, perpetually young poet whose writing is driven by equal parts idealism and original thought. A Lord Byron who grew up in the 1950s in Auburn, Alabama, negotiating curbs and gutters on his Western Flyer with baseball cards making a lovely racket from the spokes.

Yes, Johnny has a poet's demeanor and a longshoreman's work ethic. He sees the world as potential scenes in a novel, or lines in a sonnet, verses in a song. He is diligent at storing sights and sounds away in a brain that could only belong to a writer, and he does more than dream gauzy dreams about it: he writes.

After forty years in the newspaper business, I can say I've known a lot of people who rolled out of bed every morning and wrote, which, of course, is what you have to do to be a writer, any old kind. Most of us newspaper drones intended someday to write differently, beautifully, when the pressure of a daily deadline was lifted, when retirement rolled out before us like a fresh calendar. Already we had mastered half the battle: the routine of writing daily.

Not many of us did. Some old reporters died within months of retirement; look at the statistics. Most retired reporters can't stand the sight of a blank page, having seen too many. A lot of us, once unshackled, relish having nothing to do with a literary schedule or stringing together words. We finally have time for long lunches and middle-class hobbies.

Johnny Williams was never a reporter, but he might have been. He has that inquisitive nature and outsider's perspective that would have made him a good one. He also has that gallows humor thing going on.

Instead, he taught English at a college level for decades. There are, believe it or not, some similarities between the two jobs, reporting and teaching. In both professions you're often dealing with someone else's words. And, many times, those words aren't what you would have written. Not even close. They are woefully inadequate, and you can't help but try and make them better. In journalism we call it "washing garbage."

Johnny washed his own share of garbage, though he's far too polite and, well, hopeful a man to call it that. He graded endless stacks of student papers, wrote obligatory articles for stilted publications, jumped through bureaucratic hurdles that minefield contemporary academia. He had, in other words, his own day-job devils that well might have interfered with his writing intentions.

Except it did not. He wrote anyhow. Johnny did not wait for retirement. He wrote in his severely-limited spare time while teaching and rearing two children. He wrote for pleasure. He wrote for himself. He wrote because he simply had to.

John M. Williams—his professional name—published a novel, wrote plays and beautiful essays for on-line magazines. He wrote sci-fi novels, a book about 1960s garage bands. He wrote a masterful collection of short stories that remains unpublished, though for the life of me I don't see why.

Now he has the time to write as well as the talent. To do nothing but write! I can only imagine what he will produce. I expect we will be hearing from John M. Williams and reading with delight what he has written. He will approach any project with those fresh eyes and hungry spirit unusual in a man even half his age. This book, for handy example, is unique to literature that involves Auburn, ipso facto, it's not all about football.

Having grown up in Auburn, Johnny remembers the town before developers and bad choices gutted the buildings and defrocked its sacred eccentrics. He remembers the feel of the place when it had that "Last Picture Show" stamp of small town verities: beauty, gossip, heroes, music.

He fleshes out the outlines of Auburn icons we recognize but do not really know: preservationist Ann Pearson, band leader Tommy Goff, dance instructor Lynn Curtis. Even his profile choices say something about the way Johnny's mind works. He writes about them with such vivid and fresh imagery it pierces the consciousness.

The fans across the football stadium are "the vile pompom-shaking roachnest...."

When Lynn Curtis visits the print shop Johnny ran in the 1980s, it "might have been Little Richard arriving at a show."

He makes us see the things he saw, from a perspective—his perspective—that is not old but wise, not cynical but careful. The boy on the Western Flyer has grown up, and the Auburn characters in this beautiful book had much to do with it. Johnny has waited, as he eloquently puts it, until "the ego is losing its muscle tone" to deliver these words.

"The rooms he kept on this earth were inside of us," he writes when visiting his father's gravesite with his own children.

Not unlike an old reporter who has seen it all, but also with the grace of a poet and informed by decades of careful reading, Johnny Williams writes and writes and cannot stop himself from writing more.

I am in awe.

Rheta Grimsley Johnson

Preface

I offer the following sketches as a random selection from my experience growing up in, living in, and remembering Auburn. In no way do I consider them, and the reader will quickly discover that they are not, anything like a common denominator of Auburn experience, if there's any such thing, which of course there isn't. They are only the view from one narrow perspective—short clips from the film, my life.

We're told it's unhealthy to live in the past, that we should live in the moment. Well, the past has moments too. I've always felt there's an art to living in the past—the only time we really can live in the moment, when there's no future to distort it. The shame is that the past does go dreamy on us, and we need to access other eyes to see it, especially those of our younger selves. How little we suspected, as children with low-mileage brains, the importance our careless experiences would have for our later selves.

It's dismaying to reflect that even as we steadily become the past we live, we forget the majority of it. But maybe that's as it should be: let the Akashic records keep up with it all, while we take the essence with us. Still, there does seem to be something redeeming not just in remembering the past, but in re-enacting its emotions and sensations and thoughts. This is what Proust tried to do, and in our own time, the Norwegian writer Knausgaard. The reader will be relieved to learn that the current writer, with his surface dog-paddlings, bears no relation to those deep-sea divers. But I understand the impulse, and admire the enterprise. It's hard to imagine a more difficult labor, or a more perfect definition of art, than their attempts to reconstruct what always is, and even reconstructed will be, *perdu*. I can't help but believe that these neurotic labors were the only way they could render Everything into its more stable Nothing, and reach the essence themselves. I can't help but believe that something analogous is true of us all.

As I consider these essays, I realize that their subject is really what seems to be my perennial one: the mystery of time—or consciousness—two ways to phrase the same thing. I drive through Auburn now, occasionally—not one, but two people driving through two towns in two eras, and that bemusement is the moment. I'm grateful for two books that have enabled much the same sensation from my armchair: Mickey Logue's and Jack Simms' *Auburn: A Pictorial History of the Loveliest Village*, now in its third edition; and Ralph Draughon, Jr.'s, Delos Hughes', and Ann Pearson's *Lost Auburn: A Village Remembered in Period Photographs*. Many of those photographs send spears of voltage into my sleeping brain. I'm also grateful to the people who shared their thoughts and memories with me, and to the helpful folks at the Auburn University Library Special Collections and Archives Department, John Varner, and especially my friend and former colleague, Jennifer Wiggins.

About half of these reflections first appeared on the blog *Like the Dew*. I have given them their original dates. "Growing Up in Auburn" was included in the collection *Chinaberries and Crows* (Solomon and George, 2012). The others never appeared, until now, but I have given them dates, too. I wrote them after my friend Rheta Grimsley Johnson suggested that I collect the old and write some new and call the whole business *Village People*.

I hope the reader, though he share nothing of these experiences, will find something familiar in them.

John M. Williams

Photographs courtesy of Auburn University Library
Special Collections and Archives Department

Rolling Toomer's Corner, 1985

Photograph courtesy of Auburn University Library
Special Collections and Archives Department

Toomer's Corner
February 23, 2011

I grew up in Auburn, Alabama, and when I was eleven and twelve I delivered the *Atlanta Journal*. At that time the *Constitution* was the morning paper, and the *Journal* the afternoon, and they both covered Dixie like the dew. I would ride my bike downtown after school to the derelict, gaping-roofed building where we rolled our papers, load up my bike, and disemburden myself, one *Journal* at a time, home.

This general location, behind the storefronts of Magnolia and College, was like the abscessed socket of a pulled tooth: narrow alleys, ramshackle buildings, a decrepit old water tower, and the exhaust blast from the kitchen of The Grille. Urban revitalization has long since transformed the blighted area into a parking deck and general respectability, taking, as usual, all the characters with it. So the place—open to the sky with catalpa trees growing up through holes in the rotted floor, and a barely protected bench with boxes of green rubber bands where we rolled our papers—lives only in memory. Almost like newspapers themselves. In the back, beside a little passageway that led out to The Bootery on College Street, a small enclosed corner served as the office of Tiger Cab Company—proprietor, Mr. Joe.

Mr. Joe resembled a cartoon tortoise in a cap I can only call unique, rumpled and vaguely military, and was an aloof but friendly man. I never knew much about him; he often had calls, and we were always in a hurry—classic missed opportunity. Now I'd give an arm to know his story. We were kids—this was the early sixties—so of course he seemed old, but I don't really know how old he was. He was stooped almost to the point of being hunchbacked, and when the pay phone on the wall outside rang, he would hurry bug-eyed from his office (little more than a closet with a small TV, a chair, a table with coffee pot, and a ton of junk—no bed—I'd give another arm to know where he slept) in a turtle-like desperate shuffle that I can remember Billy Hodgkins expertly and most uncharitably imitating. Mr. Joe would answer the phone, jot down a note, then get in his 1953-ish Ford with a little "Taxi" roll-sign on top, which vehicle comprised the fleet of Tiger Cab Company, and off he would go.

The fellow paperboy I remember best was a lively, very funny black kid named Holy Shoulders. We had a lot of fun, but of course once we went our separate ways from that dump we never saw each other. At that time, I admit I never thought much about his name, but I've often pondered it in the years since. I always half-consciously assumed the reference was to his tattered shirt, which would have been "Holey Shoulders." But maybe there was something sacred about him that I didn't know about. Or maybe "Wholly Shoulders" was meant, whatever that meant. Could it have been an exclamation? "Holy Shoulders, Batman!" I just have no idea, and though I certainly hope Holy Shoulders is flourishing somewhere, for me he is lost in the mists of time, just as I am to him.

Papers rolled and loaded, out I would go like a tanker out of port, behind the David Lynch-like Pitts Hotel, where Olan Mills would set up shop in a creepy room, down the alley between Auburn Hardware (which, having somehow escaped the jackboot of Wal-Mart, miraculously survives), and that fried chicken-smelling exhaust from The Grille, past Mr. Hill's jewelry shop (he's still buying gold), to the corrugated metal side of Toomer's Drugs, where I would lean my tanker against the wall beside James, the delivery man's, Cushman. In Toomer's I would get a cherry or vanilla Coke, occasionally a lemonade, which was often prepared by the gracious and affable James himself who was lame and wore a leg brace and drove that Cushman all over town, God rest his soul, and maybe get a roll of Butter Rums, then head out to my afternoon's labor.

Catercorner to this spot stood the portal to the University (just recently in those days promoted from Alabama Polytechnic Institute), flanked by two oak trees, which, as always with oak trees in a normal world, I never conceived of taking any way but for granted. Back then, the tradition of rolling those trees with toilet tissue after Auburn victories had yet to evolve, and so the trees, dating to the 1800s, I hear, just stood there in their indifferent venerability. Recently, and I confess the thought was too farfetched to have occurred to me before, the claim that those trees got rolled when Bear Bryant died in 1983 entered the air. No doubt there were some Auburn people who didn't let that opportunity for tackiness slip, but that didn't happen—because I lived in Auburn at that time and remember it well; if it had happened, I would have been disgusted, but all I remember feeling that day was an odd and unexpected sense of sadness, and awe. It's very strange, the relationship Auburn people have with the Bear. Our villain. A love to hate him sort of thing—everybody knew he was a great coach.

This was twenty-eight years ago and nothing can change it—especially not a piece of sociopathic trailer trash with a bucket of herbicide.

Toomer's Corner, 2016

Photograph courtesy of Marian Carcache

Woodfield Drive: Ginger, Me. Stick Horse, 1957

Woodfield Drive: Ginger, Me, Greyhound Bus, 1956

Growing Up in Auburn
2012

Auburn, Alabama—that's my hometown. It's not mine anymore, but from the late fifties through the early seventies it was my and my fellow froglings' pond. I know that many of us, my fellow froglings and I, consider ourselves winners of some cosmic lottery to have been placed there, at the time we were, for the communal drama of our coming of age. As a college town, it was buffered from the abyss of small town hell. Intelligent, educated people were around, big acts occasionally passed through, on certain fall Saturdays the population quadrupled in a bizarre frenzy, and we had liberals. Yet at heart it was still a small, sleepy town whose frontiers, in every direction, quickly surrendered to the rural south.

The fact is, there was a fragile balance. Intelligent people, higher education itself, generate the air of possibility; and sleepy towns force the imagination inward.

The mythic quality of Auburn in my memory, correcting for enhancement, I believe derives from its mythic quality in reality as I grew up there. We created our own world as children, and that must explain why it all still seems so near to me; it was largely within all along.

Woodfield

I was born in Montgomery, and my family moved to Auburn when I was an infant. My father worked for Alabama Power Company, and when an opening came up in Auburn, he jumped on it. I have always considered this decision critical to the fortunes of our family—it was a move that put us in a position to ascend on that great upward-sloping terrain of middle America.

We settled in on Woodfield Drive, in a flat-roofed, bamboo-plagued, pecan tree-shaded house we rented from the aptly named Mr. Porch. This house, and the mystique-drenched yard that surrounded it, were my world until I was seven. I cruised those environs in Adamic wonder, as some brooding, protective spirit looked down from above. I had a stick horse that I loved, whose head was a soft stuffed tube with eyes, ears, mane, etc. Other kids had only those little plastic-headed ones that I viewed with the four year old version of the emotion that would later sour into disdain.

A fence ran round the yard, and there were certain spots where I would position myself. Naturally, in my memory I see it all from those perspectives. At the far back northeast corner I could gaze in one direction to woods that could only have stretched a couple hundred yards to Virginia Avenue, but to me seemed like something worthy of Lewis and Clark; and in the other, to a field exalted with crimson clover in spring, and pecan trees, to the back reaches of the Guytons' house where there were rabbits in wire pens. Professor Guyton, some years Daddy's senior and his fishing buddy, was a colorful nut. They don't call you "Goofy" for nothing. I don't even know what he taught, horticulture or something, but I remember my uncle's story about him from when he was in college. A student asked Prof. Guyton how the grade would be determined, and he explained that he would count the main exams such and such a percent, average in the daily quizzes, the classwork, with the labwork counting so much, and "then give you what I damn well please." I remember the day he caught a twelve-pound bass, and how huge that monster was.

Another favorite spot was on the west side of the yard, by the Graves' house. The fence, square wire on metal poles, was detached there and habitually collapsed to the ground like a loose sock, and must have been too much trouble to fix because all anybody ever did was yank it back up and prop it on the pole where it stayed about as long as a pulled-up loose sock does. So it was a certified "low place" that I was warned to stay away from, like the sinister, junk-crammed garage where you could get *worms!*, but please, I was three or four. Inevitably, one afternoon I slipped out and headed off into the beguiling unknown. In other words, when Mama conducted her next periodic check—just that fast!—I had disappeared. Auspiciously, Ginger, my beloved Ginger, half boxer, half blimp, who would snorfle her bowl of food in a single breathtaking spasm of ingestion leaving exactly the polished chopped onion pieces from the salad, was gone as well. Mama (they tell me) went into full panic. Daddy and his co-workers were summoned and the neighborhood combed. I was found in a wooded area up the street by Mr. Straiton, Ginger in faithful attendance. Good ol' Ginger.

I remember riding in the car with Mama. We had a fifty-something Buick I had a bad habit of enlisting as the main prop when I played "gas station man," using sand for gas—even caught, *in flagrante delicto*, in the background of a home movie—and in this pre-seat belt era I would stand on the middle of the bench-seat beside her. At any sudden stop or swerve her guardrail arm would swing over, a reflex she kept as long as she drove, though the toddlers evolved into various Chihuahuas and eventually nothing. I can call back the feeling of sitting in the little kid seat on the grocery buggy as Mama went up and down the aisles of the A&P, when it was on South Gay Street. That smell! The produce and Eight O'Clock coffee (or the bizarre and suspicious Bokar or Red Circle)—a smell that migrated with the store up the street in the mid-sixties, and played evocative havoc with me when I worked there in '69 and '70. I remember Mr. Tidwell (father of my classmate Mike, and later my boss) and mother-hen cashier Mae MacHargue (later a chirping scold as I bagged on her checkout lane). Leaving, we would drive around the building, past a belching vent in the narrow alley between the store and a marvelous old house half-digested by southern flora, which upon the death of the inevitable widow became a hippie nest through the early seventies, then at last fell victim to that most distinctive of Auburn traditions: the razing of the old, gracious, and beautiful, and replacing it with the vulgar, tacky, and dreadful.

For a convenience store, in that pre-convenience store world, we had Southside, or as I believed it to be until I learned to read: Sow-side (later The Gnu's Room). I remember the milk coolers in the back, Mr. Wright, the butcher, the creaking wooden floors, the front corner of exotica, including snails and (who of us ever forgot?) chocolate-covered ants, the two checkout lanes with towering cigarette racks above the cash registers, and, of course, Mr. Storey, the bustling, congenial proprietor and father of my classmate Austin. It was something of a milestone when I got old enough to go in for the milk or bread myself, Mama waiting in the car, and I can remember being puzzled when I had the exact change, because I thought the whole point of going through the line was to get money back.

I can't say how my brother Chuck, three years my senior, dealt with my arrival, with resistance undoubtedly, but when my sister Carol was born when I was four, I remember my feelings of jealousy and resentment. I would go to her crib, with its slowly-twirling songbird mobile, when no one was looking, and pinch her. Okay, that's bad—but sue me, I'm human. I didn't give up being the center of the universe without a fight. I remember my grandmother coming from Notasulga (where Granddaddy had the Methodist church and several satellites) to help Mama, who had her hands full.

Mama. Naturally, the Significant Other of that realm. When I close my eyes and think of her, I see a slideshow of her whole life, all the way to the Parkinson's-ravaged end, but definitely then: twenty-five and beautiful.

That's who I see walking down Mrs. Meagher's bumpy brick driveway the day I started kindergarten. It was the second, after birth itself, of life's serious traumatic experiences. I screamed in all the terror of primordial separation, as Mrs. Meagher said, "I've got him, Mama, go ahead," and held me—pinned me!—as Mama, her face seared with love's anguish, disappeared down the hill. When she came back to get me at noon, I didn't want to leave—so as traumatic experiences go, it was brief. I will never forget Mrs. Meagher, nor her comic handyman husband, Red, nor her schoolmarm bell, nor that little kindergarten room, the green file boxes with our names written on them in nail polish, the apple juice and graham crackers, scissors, paste, and everything else. Nor the playground with its sandboxes and swing sets and monkey bars. That first distressful day, I was given the diversionary task of counting the trains that went by. The tracks passed right behind the kindergarten, not even a block from the station. I forget how many there were, but I do believe that is where I developed my love of trains. To this day I feel a shiver when I hear one, and still watch in awe as one passes (I'm one of the few people in the world who considers having to stop for a train a lucky break)—even if they are only freight trains. Because it was the passenger trains, of course, that gave me the thrill. Those blue West Point Route engines—the blue or silver cars with the cool green windows. I can still see them sitting there at the station, hissing and purring, and I remember looking at the profiles of the passengers behind the windows, wondering how anybody could be that lucky. But I don't think I philosophized too much when I became one of those profiles as we rode to Montgomery then caught the L&N Hummingbird to Mobile to visit our cousins, at how the fulfillment is not only not as good, but isn't even the same category of thing, as the longing.

Mrs. Meagher held a reunion every year for her high school-graduating alumni, and when our turn came, I had to get special permission to take off a couple of hours from the A&P. Of course, Mr. Tidwell, that Pall Mall-smoking Jackie Gleason lookalike I can still picture in Santa Claus costume on a fire truck, let me. There's a group photo somewhere. An embarrassingly rich number of those people became lifelong friends.

One more story from the Woodfield days. 1957, a couple of years before we moved. Next door to us lived the Macons. Two slightly older than me, beautiful girls, a mom I don't recall, and the dad, Nat Macon, who was a physicist or mathematician, I'm not sure which. This may have been the first time I heard the word "genius"—which he may have been, or it may have just been blue-collar code for "real smart." He took us out in the yard one night and showed us where to look, and sure enough, right where he pointed, not to mention when, a little star silently sped across the arc of the night sky. Sputnik. I remember when I heard the Russians had launched a dog into space—who wouldn't be coming back!—I pictured Ginger in there all hooked up with tubes and wires, looking out the window, thinking *where did they go?* The Macons moved soon after that—he to some kind of hot-shotdom in Washington, if memory serves.

Brookside

When we were building our house on Brookside Drive, almost exactly to the lot a block away, we kids would go down there after hours and snoop around, and play with the lumber scraps, and build little structures of our own. A big water oak stood just behind the house, and towers there to this day, three-pronged and shading the lives of strangers. My God, that I've lived to say that.

I remember vividly the sense of freedom and possibility and immunity from prosecution of childhood. On a typical Saturday morning, if we didn't go to the kids' show at the Tiger Theater for six Golden Flake wrappers and six Coke caps that we would fish out of drink machine receptacles with a magnet on a string, I would rise pretty early, get some breakfast while those early bad generic westerns were on, maybe watch a few cartoons, then meet my pals. My best friend of early childhood, and the barefoot prototype of the genre, was Grady Hawkins—though the "best" umbrella would have to include Sharon Rouse and Wells Warren. In fact, somewhat later, Sharon, Wells, and I comprised the sole membership of the "Three Best Club," a group as tough to crack into as Augusta National. On those mornings, we would often have a debate, which could grow contentious, over how to fill the approximately twenty hours until lunch, not to mention the forty hours after. Sometimes we would draw in the sand of Sharon's driveway, perhaps pick someone to spy on, or put somebody's head in a sack, spin them around, then lead them circuitously to some spot and have them guess where it was—always a mile off. Evenings, we often played Kick the Can, with a ball, squeezing every photon of light out of the day. But mostly we would gravitate toward one of our alter-universes—either the lot sandwiched behind our houses, where we built forts, one of which was Ft. Brooksam (amalgamation of Brookside and Salmon)—later, Brookswam (the "w" for Grady's Woodfield), another, The Professional Nasty Center. I'll leave that to your imagination.

Or we would head down to Gay Street, and Salmon's Pasture.

Professor Salmon, neighborhood mogul, who lived on the corner of Brookside and Wright's Mill, owned all the land around there. I remember him as a brisk, purposeful man in a hat, and Mrs. Salmon, who survived him many years, as a nice enough, but rather aloof and intimidating lady. He had apparently thought to go into the dairy business at one time, and in the "pasture" stood a silo, a dairy barn, and a big open-sided barn full of agricultural equipment—all of it long abandoned even then. On the end of the dairy barn grew a grove of chinaberry trees, whose green berries made excellent slingshot ammo, a fact which led to the founding of the Slingberry Club and some epic wars. Another entry-point into that world was the raised sewer line on South Gay that you walked, over the creek, to a terminus in the woods. We spent hours, years, in these places, damming the creek, catching crawdads, making purple privet berry juice, building forts, losing ourselves in a cosmic web of make-believe that would seem extraordinary except that it was ordinary. The Vanderbilt Man, a Frankenstein-like figure, roamed these environs, as did The Girls—a tribe of ruthless, Amazonian females with a penchant for capturing and undressing you. You never knew, on any given day, what you might run into.

Growing up in a college town, one absorbs those rhythms and, I've discovered, never really shakes them. "When the students are gone," "the students are back," the general rise and fall of quarters (now semesters)—these are indelible categories to the natives. Along with that distinctive explosive roar coming across town on Saturday afternoons, and the blare of KA parties at night. And, often poignantly, people moving in and out. During this period our next-door neighbors were the Russells—baby Jay, my pal Rusty, the unforgettable Erk, and Jane, his wife. They ran their window air conditioner year round. Down on South Gay lived the Dooleys—and they all left Auburn for Athens (and Statesboro) and their own fame at the same time. Years later, when I was running a printing business in Auburn, my landlord was Bobby Freeman, who had played at Auburn with Vince Dooley and a little after Erk Russell, and I sat for hours listening to him talk about those days and his later career in the NFL.

While we're at it, a couple more football references—we're talking about Auburn, after all. The year 1963 was a great one for Auburn, and I was a transported, walls-covered-with-newspaper clippings, eleven year old fan. My buddy Grady Hawkins and I especially idolized Jimmy Sidle and Tucker Frederickson, and sometimes rode over to the practice field. One day (actually 1964, I believe), we were hanging around there, and went into the Field House on the north end of Cliff Hare stadium, and were standing in the hall by a water fountain. I will never forget this: out walked, in full pads, number twelve himself: Jimmy Sidle. Mr. Roll-Out. He was huge! He had that famous facial tick. I was speechless, but Grady, braver, asked him how his knee (I think) was doing (he had a recent injury), and Sidle made some polite response, drank some water, and headed out to the field.

We had brushed shoulders with greatness. The news of his death several years ago made me sad.

My friend Bill Beckwith, whose father was Sports Information Director, though I don't think they called it that then, once got me a piece of notebook paper autographed by the entire 1963 team! Sidle, Frederickson, Bucky Waid, Bill Cody, Doc Griffith, Woody Woodall, and all the rest. I've lost it! I've also lost the couple of chin straps I had—those puffy white ones the players wore then and that we stormed the field at the ends of games to get. We had gotten in by selling programs or cokes. I remember the pervasive smell of whiskey and the billion whiskey bottles in the student section. All a thing of the past.

I started delivering newspapers too in the sixth grade, and if I may be indulged in getting ahead of my story just a year or two, when I was throwing *The Birmingham News* one leg of my route was the dreaded upper Woodfield, a steep curving hill which to a kid on a bike loaded like a C-5 was formidable. I had several customers up there, including the Jordans. When I "collected," I dealt with Mrs. Jordan, whom I remember as a gracious, cheerful lady, but once, I was ushered into the den to have things squared away by the man of the house. And there he sat, memorabilia around him, basset hound at his feet: Shug. I would like to say I remember that day vividly, but I don't. I just remember his presence, which was relaxed, gentle, and warm— with some humor.

One of Shug's coaches was Gene Lorendo, whose kids, Cam, Mac (deliberate palindrome? I always wondered), and Leah, were about our age, and whose wife, Jane Lorendo, was my Cub Scout den mother. She is one of the most amazing women I ever met—in the world of crafts and hand-work, she could do anything, including carry on a fully-engaged conversation while knitting, without looking, at the speed of light. Amazing. They lived in one of those houses at Graves' Amphitheater, with a gigantic loom on the porch, and two German Shepherds: Vandy and Weagle. Once, they had a litter of puppies and that's where we got our beloved Rex. What a dog. Mama and Daddy were in Sunday school one Sunday morning, a mile from home downtown, and a fire truck came by blaring its siren, Rex in full pursuit. He got cancer in his leg when he was only seven or eight, ended up having the leg amputated, and lived another year or so, only a little impeded, with three. When he was very sick I went over to the Small Animal Clinic and got in the cage with him.

JFK got elected President and they said he was the youngest ever at what seemed to me the Methuselean forty-three. Then came the Cuba business and the H-Bomb scare. The A-Bomb was one thing, but the H-Bomb! I remember inspecting a sample bomb shelter at Neal Ingram's Amoco station, and contemplating where in the back yard we could dig the hole to put it. We made lists of what we would need inside there, and along with everybody accepted the grim reality that if anyone tried to get in, you'd have to shoot them. Americans always pull together in a crisis.

Where was I when I heard President Kennedy had been shot? In Mrs. Green's sixth grade class. Of course I remember it. She was called out, came back in, hardly able to speak, and told us: "The President has been shot." School was dismissed. For the first few hours the news was that he was in the hospital, they were doing all they could; nobody knew then that the back of his head had been blown off. There followed that surreal sequence of Walter Cronkite, LBJ, Jackie, Oswald, Ruby, funeral cortege with John John walking alongside. None of us suspected, of course, how the world was about to change. My generation seemed primed for the cataclysmic. We absorbed that cataclysm which, like all the ones to follow, became a part of us.

Early the following year we decided we needed nicknames. I remembered a kid from somewhere around there nicknamed "Beetle," and I liked that, so I announced I would henceforth be "Beetle." "Oh-h-h," scoffed Bill Dyas, "trying to be the beetles." The beetles? What was that? The word didn't have an "a" yet. As always, I was the last to know. Of course, I was soon to find out. Like all the other gazillion people, I watched them on Ed Sullivan. I've tried—with students, my own children (both big fans)—to explain it, and I can't. You can adduce all the sociological, psychological, whateverological explanations you want, and there's still no way to account for, or understand, that million-volt thrill that went through you at the sight or sound of them.

Ginger got terminally ill not long after that. The plan was for Mama to take us kids to her sister's in Mobile while Daddy handled the sad business. I remember saying goodbye to Ginger—singing "All My Loving." The words fit too well. My first love song—to a dog. I couldn't bear to listen to that song for many years after that; now it's one of my most beloved: not only does it evoke the memory of Ginger, but it was the first song any of us ever saw the lads play.

If you drive down South Gay Street today you will see a silo standing incongruously in a walking park. You will not see the long-lost world that once enveloped it. That world is a ghost, living only in my and a few other people's mental closets. I occasionally pass the place today on a road that didn't exist in my childhood, glance at it, but never feel nostalgic. It's as though the silo had been lifted from its original place, and set down in some other—which in a way it has been. I realized one day, it's not in a different time, but in a different place—in fact, they are the same. Everything is expanding; the world is not where it was. I seek refuge sometimes in that world, but more often in the even older world, the weightless world with its radiant maternal spirit, of Woodfield, and simply float there, drifting from spot to spot. And now I know who was looking down on me the whole time. It wasn't God, or a guardian angel—it was me. Well, maybe that is a sort of guardian angel. I basically agree with Wordsworth: I was closer to the stuff from which all this comes—certainly a spiritual existence, compared to *this*.

Well, anyway, I believe I've taken the story to 1964. I would be twelve in August—the president had been killed, the Beatles were upon us, and the world would never be the same again.

Lynn Curtis, circa 1950s

Photograph courtesy of Auburn University Library
Special Collections and Archives Department

Dancingly Yours, Mr. C

March 8, 2011

My father died in 1993. It was an event which created not a, but *the*, chasm in my life—the one separating Parts I and II. Part I seems somehow more real to me—as I stand here in Part II where the ego is losing its muscle tone, dissolving into my past selves and the people I love. Daddy, a mild temperament stretched over a steel frame, was aware of Lynn Curtis, and like all his power company, gas, telephone-type buddies, and everybody else I knew in Auburn, accepted him. I'm sure I don't know the half of it, but I was never aware of anyone harassing him, or making an issue of him. He was just part of Auburn. And this as far back as I can remember—the mid if not early 60s, or before.

I don't know when Lynn Curtis came to Auburn, and that he *had* come was a given—rumor had it, from New York where he had been a dancer in his youth. Nor do I know *why* he had come here. Doubtless there are people who know these answers—not I—I do not claim to have known him well. I offer only this peripheral view.

My mother, who worked for many years at Glendean Drugs, even at the original location, like everybody else around there, knew and liked him. It was hard not to; there wasn't anything defensive about him. He simply *was himself.* He was not defiantly himself; he just *was himself*—without apology or even the need to suspect one might be needed. He lived just down the road from Glendean, on Glenn Avenue, and as he didn't drive he often cut a colorful figure walking that path, his jet-black coiffure big and radiant. Made you think of Liberace. And when you saw him up close there was something thrilling about him—older than he appeared at a distance, and vivid. I realize there are places where he would not have stood out especially, but in Auburn at that time, he was unique. Why he was *here* instead of *there*, I have no idea.

He was just Lynn Curtis, and he ran a dance school.

It was not until the '80s that small town osmosis provided me with more information. I found out from my friend Brian Upright, who ran the Pet Stop and did handyman work on the side, and had done a good bit for Mr. Curtis, that the dance school, which was in Mr. Curtis's house, was lucrative and he had a lot of money. I don't guess that's really surprising; I'd just never considered it. Then from the woman who was cutting my hair at the time, whose name has drifted out with the tide, I learned that every summer Lynn would treat a group of women, his girlfriends, hairdressers and the like, to a trip to the beach. My haircut lady had been on several of these junkets, and said they had a ball. I find it fascinating to try to picture this: the daiquiris, the food, the long thin cigarettes, the raspy laughter, the card games, the glorious girlie mess in some condo—who knows? And the husbands, to whom Lynn Curtis posed no threat, doubtlessly appreciated this annual contribution to their sanity.

My next advance in knowledge of him was, I felt fortunate, personal. In the mid-80s I owned and ran a printing shop in Auburn, Village Printers—and one day a big car drove up, and what might have been Little Richard arriving at a show, but was Lynn Curtis arriving at Village Printers, emerged from the back seat in a white ensemble with a shoulder bag, and came inside. He was a charming man. No doubt most of us are charming in brief encounters—I couldn't follow him into all the corners of his life, or all his moods—maybe he had seasons of dark depression, maybe he was a tyrant to his students—I don't know! I was never really interested in his private life; I guess I was more enthralled by the myth of him. I really liked him. He was colorful, ebullient, just the right amount of self-deprecating, and he seemed more interested in my shop with its embossed tin ceiling and odd machines than in the task at hand, the printing of his spring dance recital program—*Swing Into Spring!* I named a price—he didn't flinch—he seemed to have no taste for arguing with petty tradesmen over their fees. He was equally careless about the program itself—he barely glanced at it when it was done. It was marvelous! The clip art—lovely! I will say I had obsessively proofread it with an eagle eye—and that *did* matter. Getting all those little princesses' names right. Not for the princesses, honey—*their mothers*! He knew I had slaved over it, bless my heart—he trusted me completely! And so he became a customer, though I rarely had personal dealings with him after that. I dealt with his secretary.

I sold Village Printers in 1986, and not too long after, left Auburn.

My father died, stranding me over here on this side of the chasm. I've rarely visited his grave, because with him so alive inside me, I don't do well with the iconography of death: graves and marble and hushed solemnity. But one day not too long ago I brought my kids there. They had never known him, but I had downloaded him into them as much as is humanly possible, and he lived inside them, too. We looked at his grave; sure enough, in spite of the severely chiseled name, he wasn't there. It was all a mere abstraction. The rooms he kept on this earth were inside of us—so we drifted away, my kids somewhere, and I to look at neighboring graves. I was immediately struck by how many of these people I knew! A cast of characters from my parents' generation, from all walks of life.

The town I had known was migrating, piecemeal, from *there* to *here*. My God—Lamar Sellers, a policeman I once as a youngster ran afoul of in some business I'm too ashamed of to confess here. I always believed he knew I did it, and was protecting my parents. So he took my secret and God knows how many others with him to his grave. Mrs. Umbach! My first grade teacher. Prototype of that era's matronly grade school teachers. A loving, strict woman who paddled us, when needed, with a bolo paddle, who rubbed a lotion on her hands I can still smell, who had a whistle that I searched the markets of the world to find a replica of, and never did. Mrs. Mignon Andrews! My seventh grade biology teacher, perpetually reaching in her blouse and yanking up a bra strap, who graded our insect collections with approving nonchalance—and if one had, let's say, glued the wings of a Luna moth to a walking stick and called it a Reticulated Sphincter Moth; or maybe, like a buddy of mine who'd had the good fortune of finding a grasshopper trapped on the curb when the yellow curb-painting machine came by, half yellowing it, put it in the box, labeling it a Yellow-Backed Dippenhopper, Mignon just took it all in, pulling up her bra strap and not breaking stride, cooing only an impressed *Mmmm*! A+!

And many others.

But the one that took me aback, because it was in a row with several others with nothing, including the company it kept, unique about it, was Lynn Curtis's:

Lynn Curtis
1926-1997
Dancingly Yours,
Mr. C

I think I'd heard he'd died—but figured he'd have been spirited away to some colorful rarefied resting place for dancers in New York maybe. Or if here—off by himself with a splendid monument and manicured grounds. But no. He was only here—permanently in death just what he'd been in life, and apparently what he'd wanted to be, a part of the community.

David Langner, circa 1973

Photograph courtesy of Auburn University Library
Special Collections and Archives Department

Football, Meaning, and David Langner
June, 2015

You don't pick your college football team: you are assigned one at birth. And, for better or worse, you're in this marriage until death. I'm an Auburn fan. Any team wearing those colors takes the field or court, I want them to win. A lot. I don't know why. The only way I've discovered to avoid that anxiety is not to watch.

Being an Auburn fan is not an easy job. We play in a tough league, not to mention in the same state as the Evil Empire. We go through horrible droughts, occasionally reach greatness, and provide, I'm sure, more cardiac arrests per capita than any other team in the country. Even Auburn's greatest teams have never been classic powerhouses; they've always lived by the thrill. I'm often repelled by the chicanery and turpitude of the powers at the top, but I know they are not a part of what has won my loyalty, which will survive not only them, but all of us.

No doubt theories abound to "explain" college football fervor—forgive me if I don't research them. I'm sure that experiencing, and explaining, something are mutually exclusive. College football devotion is visceral, there is no thought behind it; obviously, if it *weren't* visceral, and equally in all the camps, it wouldn't be worth watching. Still, if I *must* try to translate the preposterous phenomenon of college football passion into some other terminology, I would say: it's tribal, and it provides meaning.

There are people who look down on the whole business with dismissive superiority. I understand that. It's not their thing. But the tribal and meaningful experience it provides, I guarantee you, unless they are sociopaths, they're getting somewhere else. Personally, I don't look down on any shared public ritual because I know they are essential to our social cohesion. Take NASCAR, for example. I don't get that at all, but I get people getting it. Or Trekkie conventions. Or Grrrl Power events. I get it—and I say, the more variety the better. We enjoy feeling ourselves parts of something communal, greater than our individuality, with clear boundaries separating Us from Them, because that's the nature of life on this earth. For ants, read Edward O. Wilson. For us, read the *Old Testament*. Read the *Iliad*. Read Henry James. Read anything. That's what people are.

The Greeks gave us the word "idiot"—by which they meant someone who couldn't see beyond himself, who was incapable of social involvement, and the word evolved its connotations of stupidity via Latin and its offspring through the centuries. Western people were primarily socially-oriented until the Reformation and the advent of market capitalism needed, and created, *the individual*. This got romanticized in the 18th and 19th centuries—by Thoreau, for example, who thought you could go off and find meaning by yourself. I don't know, maybe you can. Maybe a subatomic particle can be something without any others around. But you'll find a lot more meaning in a stadium—even if, when the game's over, we have to return to our competitive, dog-eat-dog selves.

Meaning. I would add it to food, clothing, and shelter. We cannot survive without some idea that renders comprehensible the vanity of all things. And I might add, without our seeking meaning in social interaction, America, or any nation so conceived, cannot long endure.

I will admit that I've grown more philosophical about college football as I've gotten older. Wins don't thrill, nor losses devastate, me as sharply as they did when I was younger and genuinely prayed for an atomic bomb to hit the vile pompom-shaking roachnest in the stands across the field. These days I get over a defeat in about forty-eight hours, and enjoy a win maybe seventy-two. Then abstraction overtakes me, and even though there are certain victories that make life better, I can't help but remember that the players are just a bunch of kids I'll never know playing a game that I actually made no contribution to. And, having followed college football since childhood, I know perfectly well two truths: your team will win, and it will lose; and the fortunes of football programs go in cycles. It's not really that hard, once your viscera return to their proper positions, to rise above it all.

I attend only the rare occasional game these days. I remember fondly being in attendance at the Auburn-Tennessee game at Jordan-Hare in 2003. Auburn had an unsatisfying season that year—some humiliating losses, but they beat Tennessee and Alabama, so there was some redemption. There was no redemption, however, for the secret plane trip of Auburn bigwigs before the Alabama game to Louisville to talk to, gag, Bobby Petrino about replacing Tommy Tuberville. It remains a putridly sordid chapter in Auburn football history. Tuberville stayed, and got even the next year, one of Auburn's greatest ever. They went 13-0, but were denied an opportunity to play in the BCS title game because Southern Cal and Oklahoma had a lock on #1 and #2 all year, and indeed ended up in the big game where Southern Cal annihilated the Sooners for the title, only to have it later rescinded by the NCAA for the kind of violations that are outrageous when somebody else commits them. I've heard rumors that some Auburn fans claim the title (they ended up #2), but surely no team in Alabama would grovel after dubious championships.

But back to the 2003 Tennessee game. I remember a particularly beautiful Jason Campbell touchdown pass to Ben Obomanu right below me—but what really stands out in my memory about that game is the big electronic scoreboard and its relentless belching forth of Auburn propaganda that actually embarrassed me. It had been a while since I'd been to a game, and I hadn't realized things had come to that.

It reminded me of an NFL game I'd once seen—Denver beating Cleveland for the AFC championship in 1987—a pretty good game, about as interesting as any NFL game ever is, not very, that ended with Elway taking them down the field at the end to force overtime and eventually win (though they'd lose the Super Bowl to the Giants). I wouldn't have thought any more about it—and truly it could have been any one of a number of games; I just happened to take note of this one—until sometime later I chanced upon an NFL Films rendering of it, in which it had become "The Drive"—complete with slow-motion snorting, close-up spirals, tundras, voice of God, and all the rest. I remember thinking, my God, it was just a game, what the hell is *this*? It's like a black velvet Van Tiffin field goal painting.

Which brings me to the next step in this wandering reflection: a vivid experience I had last fall (2014). I attended the Auburn-Georgia game on November 15 in Athens.

Amazingly, excepting Legion Field and its atomic bomb fantasies, this was the first, and still only, Auburn game I've ever attended outside Jordan-Hare—a deep foray into enemy territory. I'm glad I went. I wanted to know what enemy territory felt like, and I had the good company of my friend Scott Smith—unfortunately a Bulldog fan, but all of his other qualities are admirable. I think everybody involved knew Auburn was going to lose, and though I suffered through the teeth-clattering, merciless fulfillment of that intuition, I was able to absorb the experience, for the first time, from a higher perspective. And I don't just mean I was in the upper deck, though I was.

The feeling of inevitability began to seep into the bloodstream about Conyers. We stopped at a gas station plaza crowded with red-accented people on pilgrimage to Athens. You could smell it then. You see, there was this issue of "last year"—in this case an electrifying last-minute gift from the gods at Jordan-Hare in a game in which Auburn had built a solid lead, only to watch it erode in a terrifying Georgia comeback: then, the ending. The divinity behind it was eclipsed the following week in an even more cosmically-intervened game against Alabama at Jordan-Hare, which put Auburn into the conference playoff and the National Championship game which, to the delight no doubt of everybody else in the SEC, they lost to Florida State, led by role model Jameis Winston.

The smell, in other words, that frigid November day, was revenge. I recognized it so well because it's in my DNA too. It is a longing for justice, to see something off-kilter rekiltered, preferably with humiliation. It is the same feeling, on the micro level, as desiring redemption for one's own life. I knew if the situation had been reversed, I would have felt exactly the same way. They don't call it the Home team for nothing. Your team represents your *home*—that nexus of formative power and meaningfulness, the locale where your self and sensibilities were formed—and you perceive that challenged. It's personal.

I realize that, as *home*, what Auburn represents to me is not how everybody else sees it—at best, a sort of conservative, provincial, yahoo decency; at worst, the clodhopper spawn of Satan. On this particular night we were the spawn of Satan.

As Scott and I made our way across campus toward the stadium, the feeling of a fine night for a public execution grew stronger. When we got to the stadium and Auburn came out, all in white, to warm up, I was stunned by the spontaneous thunderous heartfelt *boo* that erupted from the Georgia crowd. It was not polite. It radiated pure hate and a deep desire for blood. Whoa, I thought, and looked nervously around. And then there was the Matrix Board. I hadn't been to an SEC rival game since that '03 Tennessee game which had shocked me with its oversized projection of pro-Auburn ballyhoo posturing as information, and so I was really shocked now at the next-generation, slick, unrelenting, Georgiacentric crowd-stoking of that Big Brother in the sky. It never stopped the entire game—a succession of high-production featurettes reinforcing the moral superiority and honorable wholesome goodness of everything Bulldog that left no doubt in that single-minded throng who the infidels were, and who the chosen of God. And then, of course, there was the announcer, who punctuated every step of the proceedings with simple and clear commentary for the slow: *no gain on the play*! (roar)—*the line of scrimmage is . . .* **still** *the 35-yard line*! (roar)—*a gain of twenty-three yards and . . .* **another** *Georgia first down*! (roar). Very strange: there's the thing happening, which I can see for myself, but accompanied by this non-stop reminder of how important it is. Fortunately I was able to see some humor in it, and was saved from indignation by knowing it would be no different at home.

Life is hard. Most people, I think, want to do the right thing, and will pay good money for somebody to tell them what that is. At level-one thinking, moral and ethical questions are easy, but at level two and beyond, where you actually think, they are treacherous and subtle. Most folks find that disagreeable. And this is what is so appealing about football and its shit-slinging support system: it stays at level-one, where it is to thinking what painting by numbers is to painting. To that bloodthirsty mob in Sanford Stadium that night, there were no fine moral distinctions to be drawn, no ethical quandaries to navigate. The good in the universe wore red jerseys, the evil white. Too much, or any, thinking would have ruined the experience—a primal breathing together as a single entity, a savage bliss that looks like mob-delirium when you see it in others, invisible and deeply reassuring when you experience it yourself. I was glad I went to the game for that reason: I got to be the fly on the wall. And I saw clearly what is not always easy to see: we feed off each other's energy and create this experience for each other. You can hate me all you want, but you wouldn't exist without me, and vice versa.

Auburn took the opening kickoff and scored—it was all Georgia after that. Yes, there were sporadic jukes of hope—*if we score here, they fumble it back, we score again, onside kick, we'll only be ten down, we're back in the game, just need a little help from the gods* (you know the inner dialogue)—but in fact we had used up our help from the gods last year, and I don't think there was anybody there, including the players, who didn't know that—and nothing Auburn did after that opening drive worked out, while Georgia moved the ball relentlessly. We walked back to the car among the RVs and tailgating tents as though through a barbecuing enemy camp. Knowing that Alabama had knocked off #1 Mississippi State that afternoon was, let's just say, no help. Our David would be playing their Goliath in Tuscaloosa the next week—and that balance sheet was a little awry too.

I'm aware that anyone who derives all his sense of meaning and self-esteem from football needs a life. For me, college football is only a facet of the big picture. But I will admit that any attempt I've ever made to derogate its emotional power has failed. If I catch even a whiff of Auburn playing ball, I crash like a junkie. It's too strong to fight. And I'm not sure what the purpose of fighting it would be. The narratives game to game are about perceptions of good and evil, cool and uncool, seeing justice done, getting one's turn, beating the odds, payback, what have you. But the larger narrative, over the years, is deeply intertwined with the meaning by which we construct our sense of self. That's why we stick with our teams for the whole ride, win or lose. The big story, with its heights and depths, suspense, turning points, despair and redemption, both accompanies and helps create our own life stories.

That's a pretty heavy weight to put on a game, and on the young people who play it for us. When you think of the extraordinary moments in football, how they resonate in the minds of countless people, each story unique, you can't help but wonder about the one story that cannot ever be like the others.

* * *

In the Auburn football memory a handful of games are legends—and of those, one still qualifies as the most amazing Auburn game ever—well, okay, it's a tie. But on one particular early December afternoon in 1972, as I and my buddies listened dejectedly on the radio—only my friend Charles Markle going *come on! we can do it!*—maybe even with a spiel running through his head—*all we have to do is block this punt and run it in for a touchdown, hold them, make them punt again, block that one and run it in, and kick the extra point*—Auburn, and a couple of players, made history.

We should have listened to Charles.

Alabama was 10-0, and ranked #2, coming in—in position for a shot at a National Championship. They were a sixteen point favorite, with their wishbone attack. They had dominated people all year, running up big scores, but a tremendous Auburn defensive effort had held them to sixteen points midway through the fourth quarter, including a critical blocked extra point by Roger Mitchell. Still, Auburn inept on offense, it appeared it would be enough, and the game a lackluster and disappointing conclusion to a surprisingly good season following the loss of Pat Sullivan and Terry Beasley when nothing had been expected of Auburn and they'd gone 8-1, the one loss a night best forgotten (as though that were possible) in Baton Rouge. Auburn finally put a drive together, stalled, and Shug opted to try a forty-two-yard field goal. We were furious at Shug! What the hell good was *that* going to do? Gardner Jett made the kick, and the Alabama fans were pissed at the wrecking of the point spread. I've heard that the Bamers had come over to the Auburn side, and were doing a conga line up and down the steps with those infernal pompoms.

Must have been an awkward walk back.

* * *

Somebody once told Brad Langner, concerning his father David: "What makes your daddy great, breaks him."

David grew up in Pell City, and graduated from Woodlawn High School in Birmingham in 1970, where he played running back. He wanted to be a running back at the college level too, but he was small, though extraordinarily athletic (he could dunk a basketball), and from the first the coaches had him pegged as a defensive back and punt returner. This was the twilight of the segregated era in the SEC, with only two black players on the Auburn team, none on defense. The two were James Owens and Thomas Gossom, who after a shaky start would become a close friend of David's.

David's father Charlie Langner had played at Auburn in the late forties, and coached David in high school. He once kicked David off the baseball team for coming to practice drunk. "He was one of the meanest people who ever lived," Brad says. When David and his brother Chuck would get in an argument, which was frequent, Charlie would say, "Y'all fight till one of you bleeds."

"That's how Dad got so mean," Brad observes. "And Grandmother was mean too." Her nicknames for Brad years later were "Turd" and "Pissant." Charlie, very much against the current of the sixties in Alabama, advocated having blacks in sports. The KKK burned crosses; Charlie responded with a baseball bat.

If that explains the meanness, David's real trademark, a particularly pure version of reckless abandon, he got naturally. "He didn't care about tomorrow or life—he was ready to roll," says Brad. As teenagers, he and his cousin Scott Langner would head out on a wild hair camping in the Sipsey Wilderness—with beer, whiskey, steaks, and not much else. "Seat of their pants—no fear of life." As a player, David was the guy you wanted in a pressure situation—he never panicked, stayed cool, never outthought himself, lived in the moment. In the rest of life, however, that translated to: "He didn't give a shit."

Recruited by Gene Lorendo for his fierce competitiveness, he headed for Auburn in 1970.

His first day in the locker room he walked in—all 5'10", 165 pounds of him—and some lineman made a remark about his size—reportedly, "Who is this little pussy?" Whatever it was, it prompted a snakestrike swing of David's helmet/shoulder pad bundle upside the lineman's head, knocking him to the floor. "When he gets up," David announced, "tell him it was David Langner."

"He was a hit-first kind of guy," says Brad.

Like the time he was playing ping-pong (at which he was very good) with some other big lineman, and sent a line drive across the table to the guy's face. The big guy took offense and proceeded to chase David around the table—no-contest—until David leapt upon the table, and kicked the guy in the mouth—who then beat the crap out of him.

"He wouldn't ever tell you about whooping somebody—he'd rather tell about getting beat up," admits Brad.

In David Langner's four years at Auburn, he never backed off from being David Langner. He could get a little rowdy, especially on the road, so the coaches paired him with his fellow DB, the slightly older, more stable Johnny Simmons. One day in a hotel on a road game, Simmons had just gotten out of the shower and David told him some girls were calling for him outside. Simmons walked over to the door of the balcony and looked out. Then David, in one swoop, opened the door, pushed him out, snatching off his towel, and locked the door. They were lifelong friends.

David had a great career at Auburn, and was named all-SEC in 1973, his senior year. They opened that year at Legion Field against Oregon State (a doubleheader with Alabama playing Cal that evening—my God, what were they thinking?)—a game that featured a bench-clearing brawl, with #28 leaping in over the top (check it out on YouTube). Unfortunately, the year ended with the Bear's revenge for 1972, a 35-0 comeuppance on the same field. In his three playing years, David had 287 interception yards, still an Auburn record. He's tied for fifth on the career interception list with twelve, eight of those in 1972. He also had 317 punt return yards, with two touchdowns, and 340 kickoff return yards. His career, and an era, ended together. Shug would retire in 1975, and some bleak days were ahead for Auburn. And SEC football, with the advent of black athletes, and its movement into ultra-big business, would never be the same.

But 1972, and two plays in particular, lived on as his defining moment. Auburn went on to beat Colorado in the Gator Bowl that year, and ended the season at #5. Alabama went to the Cotton Bowl and lost to Texas and ended up #7. Alabama had already accepted the Cotton Bowl invitation before the Auburn game, and the Bear had famously remarked: "I'd rather beat that Cow College than beat Texas ten times." In fact, the self-described "simple plowhand from Arkansas" never beat Texas any times in his career at Alabama. (He beat them once, at Texas A&M, in 1956). As for those two plays, David always felt they overshadowed the rest, and that people didn't remember his entire career.

But such is fate.

He was drafted by the Kansas City Chiefs, and the Birmingham Vulcans of the WFL in 1974. The Chiefs offered him $13,000—but he had a bad shoulder, and was already making more money in the car business, so he passed on a pro career and embarked upon the itinerant, checkered, five-times married rest of his life.

"He wasn't scared of change," says Brad. "We bounced around." David could get mad, load up and leave a job in the middle of the night as soon as look at you—and it is exhausting to consider all the different things he did, and places he lived, to make a living over the next forty years—everybody knowing who he was at every stop. Being David Langner, he discovered, was useful.

He worked in the car business, retail and wholesale, he opened restaurants, he went into business with Bob Newton selling trailers and running a restaurant. He once worked in electronics retail in Mobile. He was hired, with no experience, by Drummond Coal Company in Walker County as an explosives technician, popular with the miners because he tended to use too much, making for less work, but also sending them diving under trucks on occasion. He was briefly a graduate assistant coach at Auburn near the end of the Barfield era, he coached at UAB, and was head coach for one year at Pickens Academy in Carrollton, Alabama. But mostly he worked in the car business, and ended up, of all places, in Tuscaloosa.

"Why Tuscaloosa?" I asked Brad.

"Oh, he loved it. He had a lot of friends there, was in a golf club. Granddaddy had some land in Gordo and when he got sick, Dad moved in. He would rather be an antagonist than hearing all the time how great he was anyway. And, you know, it's more redneck there, and Dad was a redneck. 'Warsh your clothes.' 'Plyrwood.'" Brad does a great impression of his father. Plus, as David liked to point out, he had at least one thing in common with Alabama fans: neither had attended the University of Alabama.

Brad's mother, Sandy, was David's first wife; they were married in 1978 and stayed married seven years. "The longest of them all!" Sandy says with her trademark laugh. She remembers one of their first dates, a fishing trip to a creek in Walker County. As they headed down the path to the creek, suddenly two snakes tangled together came writhing towards them. David took off running, got to the truck first, leapt in the driver's side, the nearest door, and closed it, leaving Sandy to run around the truck and get in the other side. "I should have known then!" Once they were going to a club in Birmingham and as David pulled into the parking lot they saw a group of guys selling gold jewelry and watches at the far end. "Watch 'is," said David, floored it, then stopped right before them, got out laughing and bought a gold watch. Sandy had met him through the dentist she was working for, one of David's best friends, Buddy Thorne. When she told Buddy they were getting married, his response was simple: "Don't do it." But they did, and when she was pregnant with Brad, David, who badly wanted a boy, would put his head on her stomach and howl. Not sure if that had an effect, but Brad was born in 1979. When Sandy first saw him, she said, "Son of a bitch! You gotta be kidding me. I go through nine months and this is what I get? A conehead David Langner?" She tells all this laughing. "David was a charmer. Everybody liked him. He was funny and had that crazy, wild, don't give a shit thing about him."

After David and Sandy got divorced when Brad was five, Brad went to live with his father. And from there his own life followed a roller coaster course. He had various hitches with his father, with grandparents, eventually as a teenager back with his mother, by then married to my good friend P. K. Buff, a renowned Auburn swimmer. But most of his tender years were spent with David. Concerning David's many marriages, a psychiatrist once told him he couldn't stay with a woman because he loved Brad too much. "But he didn't always take care of me the best he could."

What was it like living with David?

"No rules."

Once, in Mobile, when Brad was in the second grade, they had a three-wheeler. Brad had been accustomed to taking taxis to school, but his daddy suddenly had an idea. "You're a big boy now," he said, "you can ride the three-wheeler to school!" Of course, with the stipulation that he park it in the woods near the school and not tell anybody. But it was too cool not to tell. Word got out, and that was the end of that adventure.

David put Brad to work early. Brad remembers his dad making turkey sandwiches in his restaurant, The Lunch Box, in Birmingham, and then sending him out with a backpack to sell them on the street. Through the years, he helped out in all aspects of the car business, mostly detailing the cars that David would buy wholesale and sell to dealers. Once they had a lot in Moody, Alabama, site of the Alabama Auto Auction, with a detailing service. They were in David's office one afternoon, David working on something at his desk, when a guy came in pissed off and complaining that somebody had taken the letter jacket from his car. David didn't even look up, just kept working, and said his guys didn't steal and nobody wanted his letter jacket anyway. "I played with Michael Bolton!" the guy added—some softball team of yore with the famous singer his teammate, and the letter jacket his token—as if to slam home his case. None of that meant anything to David. He just kept working, and repeated that nobody stole or gave a damn about his letter jacket. But the guy didn't let up and Brad, watching his father, saw his bottom teeth jutting out over his top—a tell-tale sign. The guy kept at it—then in one motion David threw back his chair, jumped on the desk, leapt, and punched the guy out.

On another occasion, at a car lot in Ft. Payne, Brad and his dad got in an argument.

What about?

"Oh, we argued all the time."

Brad was sixteen or seventeen, and furious over something. He charged David, who calmly took the cigarette out of his mouth, threw Brad down, and twisted his face in the gravel. Unchastened, Brad got in a Camaro 454 on the lot, and roared away spraying gravel all over the other cars. David hopped in Brad's old Porsche and chased him down. When he caught him, he got out and said, "Take your own damn car." (Rendered in that pitch-perfect impersonation.)

David's best friend in life was probably his grandmother. Granny was certainly his biggest fan. She attended every game, and some practices, and was known to deal with the less than appreciative people around her with her umbrella or purse. Once when David and Brad were living in Homewood, David needed Brad to drive to downtown Birmingham to pick her up. Nobody seemed too concerned that Brad was fourteen and had never driven in Birmingham traffic before. Of course, he'd been *driving* for some time. Off he went, about 5'4", in a brand-new showroom Nissan 300ZX, oblivious to the blind spots, changing lanes, cutting people off, getting honked and yelled at, and picked her up. The return trip was no better, a succession of hair-raising, high-speed close calls. When they got back, David asked Granny how it went. "He did real good," she said. David took care of Granny at the end of her life.

Then there was the time there seemed to be some misunderstanding over a girl Brad had taken over to a friend's house. The misunderstander, an oversize bad-ass, showed up, wanting in. Brad, built like his father, called him and said, "This bad-ass guy is here at the front door wanting to come in and kill me! What do I do?"

David's counsel was immediate and sensible: "Is there a back door?"

Toward the end of his life, in 2012, David (who had his first heart attack at forty-seven), had to have a kidney removed. The day before the surgery he married his long-time companion Toni, to ensure she would be secure if something happened to him. Toni was the love of his life, the one woman who could put up with and handle him. He proposed by saying, "I've been married four times. I really liked each one, but I always felt trapped by a woman. You want to get married?" After the operation, Brad went in to see him and asked him how he felt. David said, "My shoulder is killing me."

"Is it the one you had surgery on?" Brad asked. David looked puzzled—and this was before he had grown addled from the cancer that would kill him two years later—and said, "Did I?"

He didn't really remember having shoulder surgery.

When he was undergoing treatment for cancer, David handled it as he had everything in life, but he often remarked that he couldn't imagine children having to go through such things, and asked everybody to donate to the Children's Cancer Research Fund.

* * *

When fellow Woodlawn alum Chris Davis ran a missed field goal back 108 yards to beat Alabama at Jordan-Hare in 2013, the extraordinary play probably struck David different than anybody else.

"I hope he handles it better than I did," he said.

Later in an interview on AL.com, he elaborated:

"It's not going to be good. He has to learn to be humble. If you've never had a reason to be in that situation before, it's tough. You make a lot of mistakes. You offend a lot of people. I certainly did and I regret it. I thought more of myself than I should have. I was arrogant and cocky. Which I really didn't have nothing to be arrogant and cocky about. It changes your lifestyle. Every time you took a step, somebody was going to tell you how good you are, and that doesn't mean anything in real life. All of a sudden you've got all these friends—or not friends—and they just want to be associated with somebody everybody knows. It's really hard to adjust. I know that now. But as a twenty-year-old kid, it's hard." (AL.com)

"Ego takes away your focus, when things come too easy," Brad explains. "He wished he'd taken a more disciplined, focused route, rather than just ride the wave. He's made me try to look ahead a little more."

Still, who knows why those two blocked punts bounced into David's hands on a December afternoon forty-two years ago? That they did was no doubt what they call luck. That they bounced into the hands of exactly the person you would have picked for them to bounce into you might argue was something else. Bill Newton said, "I always said I was thankful it was him and not a defensive lineman, who probably would have just fallen on it." David always gave the credit to Newton, a walk-on at Auburn who had blocked the two punts—even if David did keep both balls.

But it did happen, and it changed David's life.

The fame may have been a burden, but one thinks of the Greek concept of *kleos aphthiton*: undying glory, our only immortality.

David once remarked, "After all the time, what everybody needs to understand is how important it is we are remembered, not necessarily why we are remembered. For the fans to know you after forty years for us is a gift you can't get under your Christmas tree. It's not an individual accomplishment. It's a team accomplishment. Everybody gets to enjoy and share being remembered." (www.auburntigers.com)

* * *

The solidarity of that team, the Amazins', lives on. They've stayed close and lost something vital when they lost David.

"Dad was very genuine, spontaneous, stoic, compassionate. He never complained," Brad concludes. "Worked the crossword puzzle every morning."

A couple more things to remember about the 1972 game:

David had a 58-yard punt return in it, and two interceptions off Terry Davis, the second one to end the game.

Greg Gantt, Alabama's punter, who led the SEC in punting for three years and played in the NFL, had been a teammate of David's at, where else?, Woodlawn. The coaches had him in a short punt formation that day, I'm not sure why. Hoping to punch it, I guess. He died in 2011.

David died April 26, 2014, and is all legend now.

And Auburn is busy this summer installing the nation's largest electronic scoreboard.

Brad Langer with dad, David, 2013

Photograph courtesy of Brad Langner

Ann Pearson in Pine Hill Cemetery, 1984

Photograph courtesy of Gail Langley

Noble Hall

Photograph courtesy of Sheild Fickman

Ann Pearson: Chronicler and Conscience of Auburn
December, 2015

She is still the resident spirit of Noble Hall, the antebellum plantation house on the north of Auburn, with its view over the rolling front grounds to Shelton Mill Road, and its metaphorical view over the town itself and its hundred and eighty years of history. She has lived the majority of her life in this house—the Frazer-Brown-Pearson Home, as it's also known—and probably knows more about Auburn than anybody. In this age of multiculturalism, transience, and exile, she is a bulwark of rootedness, scion of eminent families, a Colonial Dame, who embodies a way of life beginning to cloud over into myth. She has a doctorate in literature, but hers is not only an academic's knowledge, it is the deeper knowledge of one who has spent almost her entire life in a place—observant and engaged.

Some people are just meant to hold the stories. She knows the people, the places, the families, the scoops, the scandals, the battles, and who's buried where. She knows viscerally how Auburn has changed. I call her a Rememberer—like a *griot* in West African culture—or a go-to source like your grandmother, who could resolve any family dispute and whose loss shriveled the possibilities of what you could know. We think of oral tradition as primitive, superseded by written, though of course they're co-existent. Ann richly represents both. We now seem to be entering a culture where everything is instantaneously retrievable in our palms, and the need to remember has become outsourced to the Cloud, along with the need to talk or listen. It must be the natural course of things, with its obvious advantages, but there will never be any substitute for the retention of our cultural identity in our human Rememberers.

Ann credits her mother with sparking her interest in local history and lore—and her mother seems a good place to begin the story.

Mary Elizabeth Duncan was born in 1903 in Bessemer, Alabama. Her mother, Annie Elizabeth Smith, was from Livingston, Alabama, and her father, Luther Noble Duncan, from near Russellville. They met while teaching at a small agricultural school in Wetumpka, and got married there in a friend's house. Mr. Duncan had graduated from Alabama Polytechnic Institute (now Auburn University) in 1900, president of his class, and in 1905, while working on a master's degree in agriculture at API, he got a job with the Extension Service, and two-year-old Elizabeth, or Libba, as she was familiarly known, moved with her family to Auburn that year. She grew up in the house her father built on Opelika Road around 1912, and attended school across the street (not a highway then) at Lee County High School. In due course, she entered API herself as a home economics major, but had no taste for school and dropped out in 1923 when her younger sister Margaret developed a brain tumor and died at the age of nineteen.

No more school for Libba. She stayed home with her grieving mother for a while, then took a job in 1925 as a mail clerk in the Extension Service, now headed by her father. In the early thirties she was briefly married, but the marriage was not successful; her husband was an alcoholic, and she got a divorce. Otherwise, she enjoyed an energetic single woman's life in early twentieth century Auburn. Among other pursuits she started a Camp Fire Girls chapter in Auburn and ran it with great success.

In 1938 she met Dr. Allen M. Pearson, an API graduate and at that time head of the Wildlife Research Unit, six years her junior. Pearson had come to Auburn from Washington County, and earned his PhD at Iowa State, where his roommate was E. V. Smith, who also came to Auburn and a career as dean of the School of Agriculture and director of the Alabama Agricultural Experiment Station. After a brief period working in pesticide research for DuPont in Delaware, where the south Alabama native didn't care for the weather, Pearson had accepted Auburn's offer to head the Wildlife Research Unit, and come back in the mid-thirties. Meanwhile, Smith had married one of Libba's good friends, and one evening the Smiths invited Libba and Pearson over for a frog leg supper. "Sometimes," Ann reflects, "if I feel too full of myself, I think: I'm the result of a frog leg supper." Since second marriages were low-key, the couple just had their ceremony at the Methodist parsonage with the preacher's wife as witness. While Libba was waiting on the front porch of the old President's Home (now Cater Hall) for the groom to pick her up, one of her old boyfriends chanced by and asked her out that night. Sorry, she said—she had a previous engagement.

Ann was born in 1941, and that year her grandfather, now president of API, bought the deserted Greek revival antebellum house on the northern outskirts of Auburn, and two hundred and fifty acres, for $15,000. In 1943, the Pearson family, with two-year-old Ann, moved into the house, and Libba spent the next thirty years refurbishing and furnishing it, and throwing herself into a variety of civic enterprises in the growing college town.

Ann was close to her mother, and remembers her as a consummate housekeeper and cook, and a tireless restorer and furnisher of Noble Hall. She hooked rugs for every room, she frequented antique shops, constantly bringing home what often looked like junk but which she refinished into a houseful of marvelous furnishings. She did the same for the Auburn Woman's Club, in a house moved from campus to Sanders Street, and for the museum of the Lee County Historical Society in Loachapoka, of which she was a charter member in 1968, even while battling for the last ten years of her life the cancer that would kill her in 1973. By virtue of her colonial ancestry (a descendent of Thomas Bond of Maryland), she served two terms as Regent of the Lighthorse Harry Lee chapter of the DAR, and was also a member of the Colonial Dames, Magna Charter, and the United Daughters of the Confederacy.

Slight, never in good health, Libba was an extraordinarily creative and accomplished woman, from whom Ann absorbed everything. "My mother preferred cookbooks over textbooks, but she was wise in things of the heart. I never knew her knowingly to do a mean or selfish thing. This isn't to say she was a saint in plaster, none of us are; she had her ideas and opinions and wasn't above voicing them in the face of opposition. But she was an unusually giving and unselfish person." Ann's father, "in a rare burst of affection," once told her, "Ann, your mother weighed only ninety-eight pounds when I married her, but she could out-work any three people around her."

* * *

Auburn was founded in 1836 by Judge John Harper, and famously named by his poetry-reading daughter-in-law. The house that would become Noble Hall was built in 1854 as a plantation house—today the only one left standing in the area, though Auburn has several antebellum town houses—by Addison Frazer, a plantation owner, lawyer, and businessman in the young town. He hired a contractor from Kentucky named Henry Foster to design and build it—which he did with slave labor. The Methodist East Alabama Male College was chartered in 1856, but the cotton economy ruled the agricultural area. Frazer and then members of his family lived in the house until 1922. For a while, after one of his daughters married Oscar Casey (Kay-zee), it was known as the Casey Place. During the Civil War, some sources say the house served as a makeshift Confederate hospital. Legend has it that Mrs. Frazer showed the Masonic sign to Yankee troops ransacking the area near the end of the war, and they took only the horses and mules. After 1922, for several years, the house was abandoned and stood empty, and began deteriorating. Students, including Ann's mother, would come out to the "Haunted House" for picnics. The haunting was real enough, though not by spirits—but by various vagrants, white and black, and chickens and assorted other fauna at loose throughout. The picnickers would often sign their names on the walls upstairs, which Ann discovered when peeling off the wallpaper at one point. She recognized the name of one of her high school teachers. Libba loved those expeditions, and it was then that she cultivated the dream of one day living there.

* * *

In 1932, Dr. J. V. Brown, head of building and grounds at the college, bought the place and did most of the major work of restoring and modernizing the house into livability. He installed bathrooms and central heat, replaced the original wooden columns front and back, which had rotted, with brick and mortar, and replaced the porches. Many students did part-time work out there during those years. When Ann's grandfather, Dr. Duncan, bought the house and acreage from Dr. Brown in 1941, he continued the restoration work. He had planned to retire there, but, afflicted with heart trouble, died in office in 1947, and never used it for anything more than a weekend house.

Ann was only six when her grandfather died, so she doesn't remember him very well, but he was a notable figure in Auburn history. Luther Duncan grew up in northwest Alabama and came to API in 1896. He eventually became involved in the college's Cooperative Extension work, disseminating information about progressive agricultural practices in the bleak economic conditions of the rural South. He was a key figure in the founding of 4-H. In 1920, he became the director of the Alabama Extension Service. Despite criticism, most notably from *Birmingham News* publisher Victor Hanson, for his linking the interests of the Extension Service a little too cozily with those of the newly-created Farm Bureau, and because of his repeatedly demonstrated organizational skills and financial acumen, Duncan first served on a transitional committee of three (the "Learned Asses," some had it), then was appointed API president in the depth of the Depression, in 1935. He fought hard for funding from the state legislature, wresting financial support equivalent to that given the Evil Empire across the state, and helped put API, and the Extension Service, on the map in a significant way. A bit of controversy still attends his legacy, but Duncan Hall and

Duncan Drive on campus attest to his influence, and his portrait hangs on campus as Auburn's tenth president.

* * *

Since she was only two when her family moved into Noble Hall in 1943, Ann has no memory of living anywhere else as a child. Today, an expanding Auburn is rapidly changing the character of the locale, but in the early forties the area lay outside the city limits and "in the middle of nowhere." The unpaved road seemed to lead forever into the north Auburn woods, and the mailman certainly didn't venture out that far. The family had to run their own private phone line, which Ann's father maintained. Black sharecroppers still lived in cabins on the grounds, growing cotton. The family had a cook, who lived in the kitchen, separate from the house, and cooked breakfast every morning at six. It was, all in all, an idyllic place to grow up, if you weren't a sharecropper—the woods stretching endlessly behind, adjoining the Pick property—and Ann spent her childhood barefoot, running around in blue jeans. "I loved growing up out here."

Ann's father and grandfather were avid hunters, and raised purebred bird dogs. Ann, a lifelong animal lover, loved those dogs and would take naps out in the yard with them. That is, until one of her mother's friends gave her a kitten when she was five—"and then it was all over with the bird dogs. I went to cats." As her readers know, she has remained an ailurophile of the first order.

During Ann's early childhood her grandfather, busy as API's president, lived in the town house on Opelika Road, but often spent his weekends in the country. Ann's father, who, unlike her mother, had always been more interested in the farm and the herd of fifty Angus cattle than in the house, stayed very busy teaching zoology at the college, and running the farm.

"I didn't know my grandfather that well," says Ann. When he died in 1947, he was succeeded by Dr. Ralph Brown Draughon. Ann's grandmother inherited Noble Hall for a life interest, moved there and lived four more years, and Ann got to know her better. A native of Livingston, Alabama, she had been an elocution major, when there were such things, under Julia Tutwiler at Livingston Normal College, and read to young Ann a lot. Ann was ten when her grandmother died in 1951, and Ann's mother inherited the house, giving it the name "Noble Hall" at that time, to honor of her father.

In the fifties Noble Hall was still a working farm, and in addition to her ongoing restoration, furnishing, and decoration projects in the house, Ann's mother cooked for all the help. When she first moved out there in 1943, she decided that would be a good time to read *Gone With the Wind* (published in 1936), and she would sit in the front bedroom reading, looking out the window at the rows of cotton stretching into the distance and think, "I'm in it." But laboring like a man, and cooking daily meals for the workers, including a number of students working part-time to earn a little money, "she wasn't exactly Scarlett O'Hara." The students, Ann remembers, would eat with "us" in the dining room, while the black workers would eat on the back porch in good weather, and in the basement in bad. In the late fifties, when he was about fifty, Ann's father developed crippling arthritis and, after running into some financial troubles, had to sell his cows. In fact, the malady would force him into early retirement from the college, though he would live at Noble Hall until he died at age ninety, in 1999. I'm not sure what he saw, or cared to see, from that vantage point, of the developments transforming the not so sleepy college town to his south. Let's just hope he never drove down South Gay Street.

In the early sixties, when Ann was a senior in college, her mother got colon cancer, though it was discovered late, and repeatedly misdiagnosed. For the last ten years of her life, though she remained extraordinarily energetic, she found it impossible to work at the level she once had, and had to hire more house help. She would succumb in 1973, and the town would pour out a chorus of commemoration at the loss of one of its most extraordinary citizens. "We loved her dearly and will miss her greatly," wrote Alice Cary Gibson in a memorial.

* * *

Ann came up through the public schools in Auburn. Naturally, she attended Mrs. Meagher's kindergarten, then started first grade at the Samford Avenue School. The swelling student population forced the temporary re-opening of Northside School (Lee County High School), where her mother had attended, across the street from the town house, and Ann went there for three years, then back to Samford, as Northside was phased out of the school system. That stolid edifice, built in 1914, became in my era the "Youth Center," next to the City Pool—still vigorous in the memory of both the current article's subject and its author—the sweaty chlorine smell of the locker room down below, the little wire baskets for personal belongings, the rectangle of Clorox-water one had to wade through before ascending the steps to the pool where "No Horseplay" was allowed—the high dive!—swimming lessons—Greyhound buses going by on Opelika Road. The author's teen band The Blue Boys played in the Youth Center in the mid-sixties, and psychedelic decoration arrived a couple of years later. Then the wrecking ball in 1973.

Overall, Ann felt she got a pretty good secondary education. As for the teachers, like all of us, "I had some very good ones and some very bad ones." Among the best she especially remembers Mrs. Miller, English; Mrs. Otis, French (and the author's long-time next-door neighbor on Brookside Drive); and Mr. Guthrie, chemistry. When she finished high school in 1959, Ann started at API as an art major. She quickly discovered, however, that nature had not intended this, and since she was doing so well in English, she almost immediately switched to that major. She credits the inspiration and encouragement of her instructor, Mrs. Faulk, for the change, and has fond memories, as do many of us, of Sara Hudson in the department, who led her to concentrate in Victorian studies. Ann enjoyed her college years, and since Noble Hall was outside the city limits, she qualified to live in the dorm, which she loved. "I wanted to be up there where the action was." Now, fifty years later, she still keeps up with several of those old roommates.

After she graduated in 1963, she headed to Chapel Hill for graduate studies, and got an MA in 1965. She came back to Auburn, where the university had just started a PhD program in English, so she enrolled, and got her degree in 1971, with a dissertation exploring Dickens' use of setting in his novels. The old guard was in its heyday at Auburn in the late sixties. The names Benson, Current-Garcia, Hudson, Wright, Madison Jones (working on one of his first books then), and Rea (in History, where Ann had a minor) come readily to her mind. After she finished her coursework, Ann headed off ABD to Americus, Georgia, for her first full-time job at Georgia Southwestern in 1968. She liked Americus—it reminded her of Auburn—but loathed the job. It wasn't just that she wasn't cut out to be a teacher—a blessing in disguise, some would say—but that the situation at Georgia Southwestern was difficult. The school had been a Normal School, a two-year school for teachers, but they were in the process of converting to four-year, and "were letting anybody in." The head of the English department, a recovering high school teacher who unfortunately retained the temperament, was "just awful." "She had us using workbooks in Freshman English!" Ann's roommate survived only a year; Ann, two. Then she came back to Auburn for good. She moved into the town house on Opelika Road, and got a temporary full-time job at the university library where she earned money to support herself while finishing her dissertation. She also taught part-time in the English department for a few years.

Those of us who lament the disappearance of Old Auburn, among other scenes of annihilation often focus on those first couple of blocks of Opelika Road—where at the turn of the century George Alfonso Wright, subject of another of these reflections, grew up—now commercial and the site of the Frank Brown Recreation Center and the Jan Dempsey Community Arts Center, which have supplanted every trace of the City Pool, Northside School/Youth Center, softball field, basketball and tennis courts. On the south side of the road apartments and businesses and the sprawling post office and parking lot have replaced the row of vintage houses. Ann's house stood in that stately row, but in the seventies the area was losing its charm. That end of Opelika Road had become clogged with traffic, she could hardly get out of her driveway, things were being stolen from her yard—and "it wasn't a neighborhood anymore." Plus, the old house needed a lot of expensive work she couldn't afford. In 1987, the post office bought the whole block to North Ross Street, and abandoned their longtime building on Tichenor Avenue, now City Hall, rich in history and personality but poor in square footage. I once had a post office box in the old building, and frequented the place, where Neal Ingram, a family friend, following his years running a service station, and his son Terry worked the windows. I remember the smell—the smell of old post offices everywhere—an olfactory trait they share with old drugstores. The modern age has stolen so many smells.

Ann finished her dissertation in 1971, and living in the aging, doomed house, she had some lean times. She had been cured of teaching, and thought that perhaps she could make a living writing. She had a small independent income, but it wasn't enough. So, at the suggestion of Rheta Grimsley, former editor of *The Plainsman*, and then working for *The Auburn Bulletin*, the progressive daily newspaper started as a weekly, *The Lee County Bulletin*, by Neil Davis in 1938, she began writing a weekly column. As for Rheta—now nationally syndicated columnist and author Rheta Grimsley Johnson—Ann admits, "I owe her one."

Ann, who had already been writing reviews and feature stories for the paper, wrote the column as a freelancer for twelve years, into the eighties, by which time she had moved over to *The Opelika-Auburn News*. Mainly inspired by her mother, and all her stories of Auburn's yesteryear, Ann embarked on the enterprise of ferreting out the stories of the town and its people. Many of us remember the countless interesting sketches of "In Random Order" in that era. All, or most, of them are collected in the Auburn University Archives, and together they are a history book. They are nicely complemented by her feature stories, most memorably profiles of the Post Office, the train depot (miraculously saved from the juggernaut of progress and recently renovated as a restaurant), The Bottle, and Pine Hill Cemetery, and her series of children's Christmas stories.

Also, in the late seventies/early eighties she got a contract with Zebra Books to write five mystery novels in their tightly formulaic mystery series. She obliged with *Murder by Degrees* in 1979, in which perky student Maggie Courtney has to help solve the murder of the odious female head of a college English department, an exercise in wish-fulfillment that is the prerogative of all writers, and a good illustration of the preferability, in most cases, of leaving the killing of department heads to books. She had to set it all up rather mathematically, provide an array of suspects and so many clues (including in the cover art), and unravel it all in the final chapter, sealed when one bought the book, requiring scissors to free the identity of the culprit. She followed that with *A Stitch in Time*, inspired by her enjoyment of needlework, and *Cat Got Your Tongue*, inspired by the obvious. At that point Zebra Books dropped the murder mystery series, and Ann never had to deliver the last two. "I was a little relieved because I had run out of ideas."

Her first column on Pine Hill Cemetery—the venerable original cemetery of Auburn on Armstrong Street, and final resting place of Judge Harper himself, Addison Frazer, and many other notables—was of special significance in her career, making her Auburn's most visible taphophile, and leading to a series of columns on the distinguished residents, and further interest in the history of Auburn. She even started a novel at that time on the subject, *Strawberry Hill*, but never completed it. Eventually, in the spring of 1996, Ann, then president of the Heritage Association, and Carolyn Levy, would adopt the idea of Lantern Tours in the cemetery, to raise money for its upkeep. Ann wrote many of the scripts for Pine Hill. Some of her information she drew from a handwritten history of Auburn by Mrs. W. B. Frazer, whose family had lived at Noble Hall. Mrs. Frazer was born in 1850, and wrote her account from memory in the 1920s. A memorable example of a Pine Hill column was entitled "Touching a Very Human Heart" and appeared in *The Opelika-Auburn News* on July 16, 1987. It tells the story of a young man in pre-Civil War Auburn, Jeff Wynn, who was killed in a hunting accident by a friend in 1859. After he was buried in Pine Hill without a marker, his devoted former slave, Amos Wynn, (I think it's impossible for us today to understand this relationship) started an informal savings account with Burton's Book Store owner Robert Burton until Mr. Burton told him he had enough to buy a headstone for his former master's grave. That marker was bought, installed, and then stolen, and has remained at large since; in 1991 Ann had a replica made from a photograph taken by George Alfonso Wright, and reinstalled. Amos Wynn would live on in Auburn until the 1920s, a welldigger and something of a town character—George Alfonso Wright remembered him from his boyhood—and then was buried in an unmarked grave himself in Baptist Hill Cemetery, with no one to return the favor—that is, until Dr. Charles Glenn heard about the story and had a marker placed which still stands. The Lantern Tours have been extremely successful from the start, and are still conducted bi-annually. The scripts of those tours, and other information about Pine Hill, were collected in the book *Auburn Sweet Auburn: History, Stories and Epitaphs of Pine Hill Cemetery 1836-2010* by the Auburn Heritage Association in 2010.

Speaking of George Alfonso Wright, Ann knew him well and remembers him as a sententious and ornery fellow. When he was in the nursing home near the end of his life, she would sneak in bourbon (until she found out from Clark Hudson that he preferred Scotch). "He'd pour a glass for himself, and one for me. I'd have to drink out of his toothbrush cup." Alfonso was well-known for writing letters—to everybody. Family, friends, celebrities. "Oh yes," says Ann. "He used to write my mother all these letters. I found a drawer full of them after she died. I tossed them."

But back to Baptist Hill, a few blocks east of Ebenezer Baptist, Auburn's first black church, founded by freed slaves in 1865 (now the home of Auburn's Unitarian Universalist fellowship). Baptist Hill was Auburn's first black cemetery, which countless cars swoosh obliviously past on the busy thoroughfare of Dean Road every day, and another key point of interest in Ann's work in this period—late eighties/early nineties. Falling further under the spell of Auburn history, she became active in the Auburn Heritage Association, serving as president for eight years, and undertook the project of cleaning up Baptist Hill Cemetery, learning about its residents, and about the black Auburn community in general.

The first thing she learned when she started the project, and would find reinforced when she undertook a similar clean-up of Pine Hill later, was that the city had little interest in the upkeep of its historic cemeteries. The second was that no one "owns" Baptist Hill. The city could declare eminent domain if it liked, but that would mean trouble and expense, so it doesn't like. It's just there. Some unknown white citizen around 1870 donated the land on the east edge of Auburn for an African-American cemetery, but no one has ever found any record of the transaction, or any information about ownership at all. Ann tried to compile a list of all the graves, but of course many are unmarked, some just indentations in the ground, and the cemetery itself never had any kind of plan. The culture of the time was little devoted to record-keeping, unconcerned with dates, and what information does appear on the markers often was painted; sometimes family members would repaint the slabs periodically, sometimes not. Burials were random; you just picked out a spot you liked, and started digging. The oldest grave the Heritage Association has been able to identify is that of a ten-year-old girl, interred in 1879.

Neither did Ann and her colleagues find any cooperation from Peterson-Williams Funeral Home in Opelika, which had handled African-American burials in Lee County for many years, and had bought out Pitts-Frazier Funeral Home in Auburn, whose records went back for decades. "They didn't want anything to do with the white folks." Ann made many entreaties to the Peterson-Williams authorities, explaining that the Association wanted to gather and organize the information to put in Archives, which would greatly facilitate genealogical research, but "they didn't care."

It would be hard to imagine a more vivid illustration of the lack of trust between the two communities.

After the clean-up Ann was rewarded in the best way when an African-American woman told her, "I used to be afraid to visit my mother's grave, but now I can." Baptist Hill still has one or two interments a year, and "there's still plenty of space."

In 1980, Ann contributed the Auburn section to the book *Lee County and Her Forebears*, edited by Dr. Alexander Nunn, Loachapoka native and longtime editor of *The Progressive Farmer* (he wouldn't take liquor ads) who founded the Lee County Historical Society in 1968. "About midway through the book, he started losing it in the head. And we had to cut my part almost in half—we lost most of the human interest stories. It was a mess getting the whole thing together with him losing it. It's not bad, but could have been so much better."

In the 1980s the health of Dr. Pearson, Ann's father, began to decline. He had been living in the big house, and Ann in the cottage out back. The last years of her father's life were a difficult time. Dr. Pearson, a man of some temper, hadn't let Ann do any work on the house—even have it painted, which it badly needed. "He was against anything ornamental. He had plenty of money, but became a miser. He wouldn't spend it on anything except his own personal comfort. If it was leaking over his head, he'd have it fixed. If it was leaking somewhere else, he wouldn't bother. There was so much work that needed to be done; I didn't have the money, and he wouldn't spend it. I had a hard time there for several years."

In 1990 Dr. Pearson fell and broke his hip; Ann moved him into a nursing home, claimed Noble Hall, and had it renovated. She's been living there ever since. She received the Roy Swayze Award from the Alabama Historic Commission for this restoration and renovation work. Noble Hall was the first structure in Lee County to be named to the National Register of Historical Places, in 1972. In 2008, Ann became the first donor to the Land Trust of East Alabama, protecting a hundred acres around Noble Hall (not including the cat cemeteries) in perpetuity. In 1999, Dr. Pearson died at age ninety.

In addition to her service in the Auburn Heritage Association, and the Lee County Historical Society, Ann has been the Lee County representative for the Alabama Cemetery Preservation Alliance, and served on the board of the Historic Chattahoochee Commission. She has been devoted to the Lee County Humane Society almost since its founding in 1974, contributing financially and in volunteer work. She served as its vice president for many years, publishing its newsletter. One organization she was involved in doesn't sit well in her memory: the Historic Preservation Commission of Auburn—with members appointed by the mayor and approved by the City Council. "It has no teeth. We didn't do anything the entire six years I was there. I was thinking about resigning, but then my term was up. The administration doesn't support it. They might as well just do away with it. A good friend of mine who was on the Planning Commission for a good while said to me, 'Ann, just face it—money and development will always win.'"

In recent years, Ann has been dealing with health issues, but co-authored the book *Lost Auburn: A Village Remembered in Period Photographs* (with Ralph Draughon, Jr. and Delos Hughes) in 2012—a heartrending nostalgic orgy for some of us. She also undertook the restoration of Sunny Slope, an antebellum one-story, hipped-roof Greek revival cottage on the south, no longer outskirts, of town, home in the 1850s and 60s of secessionist and publisher William F. Samford, and childhood home of his son William J. Samford, Alabama governor and namesake of Auburn University's defining building. "I just did it to save the house—I didn't have anything in mind to do with it when I did it." The restoration turned into a million dollar project, recently finished. "I talked to the city to see if they had anything they'd want to use it for, but Bill Ham [Auburn mayor] was totally uninterested. So I made a deal with the university: I've given them a legacy donation; they won't get the deed until after I die. But in the meantime I'm leasing it to them at no charge. They pay utilities and taxes, but no rent. I hear they're going to use it for OLLI classes, which is fine. But if they do anything out of line, they ain't gonna get it."

Sunny Slope was listed to the National Register of Historic Places in 2009. I remember romping around there as a kid with my buddy Bobby Emrick, whose family, I learned, bought the property in 1890—not that I knew it then. It was just a wonderful locale and old house (hardly a cottage) where we played and listened to Dave Gardner records. Bobby had about the coolest thing, to me at that time in my life, one could have: a Honda S-65. In recent decades, subdivisions have been closing in for the kill.

We can all thank Ann.

* * *

Ann shared with her mother a love of needlework, and of Auburn history and a dedication to preservation—if not a love for cooking, keeping house, and an aversion to school—and both have fought the battle to find the right balance in Auburn between preservation and development. Ann's view of how that battle has played out is clear: "I don't like what Auburn's been turned into. It's been over-developed. Seventy-five foot buildings are not in keeping with the rest of the town. And we don't need student housing in the middle of town. Talk to most city politicians about local history and you just see their eyes glazing over. And come hell or high water they're going to have that hotel built where the city parking lot is. I don't care how many people object."

There is indeed such a project in the works, and plenty of objectors. The city should have renovated Pitts Hotel many years ago.

Many would ask, why pour money into an old building or house built for the needs of another era, when you can tear it down and put a bigger, better, more efficient one in its place that will accommodate more people and generate more revenue? I can only say, the world is divided into people who think that's a good question, and those who think only a Snopes would ask it.

I recognize that much of my personal attitude is nostalgia, a preference for the world that formed me, and I'm only trying to hold onto it as a new generation restlessly goes about replacing it with its own. The obliteration that wipes the earth's slate clean of us pains the heart—but curses the present with vulgarity and shallowness. Preserving the best of the past and letting it gracefully co-exist with the progress of the present expands the timeline of our life experience from the fleeting to the ancestral, and imbues our environment with a richness and depth no amount of new condos and smartly landscaped chain restaurants can ever atone the loss of.

Ann has spent a good part of her life fighting this fight.

What does she miss the most as she looks back over her life in Auburn?

"Dime stores. And people. I used to know most everybody. I went to an event recently—there were two hundred people there and I just knew a handful of them. I go in restaurants—I look around—I don't see a soul I know. I ask myself, who are these people?"

I've asked myself the same question many times. In fact, they are Auburnites—perhaps unaware of what Auburn was, perhaps uninterested—but in control of what it becomes.

Photograph courtesy of Gail Langley

Auburn High School Band, circa 1968

(Me, first drummer in the row)

Mr. Goff, circa 1960s

Mr. Goff
February 2, 2014

Mr. Goff. Not "Tommy Goff" or "Tommy" or some dorky nickname—Mr. Goff didn't have nicknames. A bandmate once made the mistake of calling him Mr. Goof—nobody ever said *that* again. No, there was nothing else really conceivable: he was *Mr. Goff.* He was the best teacher I ever had, and one of the handful of truly extraordinary people I've met in life—and a legion of former students scattered over the world would say the same.

Mr. Goff remains as one of the indelible sentries standing guard over the first era of my life—that epoch of the 50s and 60s that's really beginning to feel like a work of fiction. When I was in the sixth grade the Beatles came out, and I became fascinated with drums. Of truly awe-inspiring phenomena in my life, one would easily be the Auburn High School marching band—that is, the column of drummers playing their cadences as the spruce corps came swaying down the street. Ken Young. Jack Marshall, James Jones (aka "Morticia"—and there *was* something cadaverous about him). And, above all, the legendary Stonewall Breyer—percussionist extraordinaire, and the first person over whom I was starstruck. My buddy Grady Hawkins and I used to march down Gay Street pretending to be drummers, and I could imagine nothing finer. Ray Havron, Bill Dyas, Joe Herbert, and I formed a rockin' combo, playing sock hops and twist parties, but the driving ambition of my life was to be a drummer in the AHS band myself.

Seventh grade—after being clawed from my mother's grasp the first day of kindergarten, the second great transition of my life. Your own locker, with a combination you had to memorize, changing classes, PE, the melding of all the grammar schools into the common pool of junior high and an entire new wrangle over the pecking order—and, for some of us, band tryouts. Half the kids trying out for band wanted to be drummers—no doubt that's typical, and an aberration quickly corrected by fate and nature. The tryouts consisted of one's having a go at the various mouthpieces, and then Mr. Goff tapping out a rhythm that one had to repeat—just hands on legs—he would no more have put drumsticks in our hands at that point than you'd put a stick of dynamite in a baby's. I passed, but so did plenty of others—the nucleus of what would become the drum corps over the next six years, as well as the pretenders: Leigh Cannon, Paula Reynolds, Gloria Liverman, and, unforgettably, Jimmy Posey with his unibrow and high-dollar drumpad. Too many idle thirteen-year-old drummers tend to be annoying if you're trying to teach a random collection of village riff-raff who have never held an instrument to make music, and we were forever being punished. Banishment outside (the briar patch). Push-ups. Running laps around the band room. I can still see Paula Reynolds' head bobbing past the front windows. That cramped building—tucked behind Samford Avenue school, band room on one end, Miss Bright's music room (more like a closet) on the other, with photographs of the different instruments of the orchestra being held by musicians who all looked like Nazi doctors—has not survived. Except in memory. Seventh period! We began to learn about music, but the drummers had a lot of dangerous down time. Once we climbed up into the attic from the shelves in the instrument room and looked down through a hole in the ceiling at our bandmates playing chorales. Neither that, nor the time we were outside and licked leaves and stuck them to our faces, and cut off twigs and branches and wedged them in our hair, glasses, belts, shoes, and pockets, then walked in, went over big.

Even then, in 1964, Mr. Goff had a nascent sense of legend about him—and it shocks me when I do the math: he was thirty-one years old! Destiny had given him a chance shot at the job in 1956, and he had seized it, done a stint in the Army in the late '50s, then come back and started putting together outstanding bands. He had an air of the military about him. The band had officers, rules, the meritocracy of chair tryouts, demerits. The last were severe, not given out lightly, and if you got one—as I did, several times—you had to play it off. For a drummer that entailed, you, a snare drum, a piece of Haskell Harr (another Nazi doctor) music, that little office with the tuning machines that looked like something out of Flash Gordon, and Mr. Goff. I can still get a little tight in the throat when I think about it. In memory I see Stonewall Breyer's trap set—oyster black pearl Ludwigs, just like Ringo's but with two rack toms—set up on the side of that small room, with strict orders not to touch them. The senior band had a Dixieland group, Stonewall a force of nature on drums, who played "Tiger Rag" at the supper concerts, one of the thrills of my life. One day fellow drummer Bill French and I found ourselves in the band room somehow alone, and I swear the devil made us do it—we each took a turn behind those things, murdering them. What a rush! If Mr. Goff had caught us he would have killed us. He possessed an innate air of command and authority. You didn't break his rules, you didn't slack, you didn't come into his environs with anything that even resembled disrespect. You, and everybody else, tried as hard as you could, and gave him something beyond what was natural. I don't know how or why. You just did. He was Mr. Goff. People who couldn't do that didn't stay in the band.

In fact, as we moved toward ninth grade, plenty of people did fall out—most of the would-be drummers, obviously, but others too, who didn't practice and didn't care. I can remember Mr. Goff using the phrase "dead wood." In need of pruning. Bill French had come from Cary Woods School—I from Wright's Mill—and in the beginning there had been a bit of rivalry between us—which lasted just long enough for his superiority to be unmistakable, about ten minutes. He was already an exceptional percussionist, as he is today. He made a much better friend than rival and I never envied, always admired, him. Our junior high band, rich in talent, achieved several firsts, including first halftime show, first playing of the national anthem at an assembly, though the latter was marred by a botched opening drum roll. The senior drum major, David Hill, I think, gave the signal, and it was one of those situations where everybody waited a fatal microsecond for the other guy to do it, resulting in an indecisive feeble patter that had to be waved dead for a second try—to that point, one of the most embarrassing moments of my life—superseded a couple of years later when we set up six trap sets on stage at a supper concert for six drum solos on "Watermelon Man" and made the mistake of letting Bill go first, who played something so mind-boggling we lost the time and degenerated into chaotic mush. I crawled to school the following Monday.

Senior band tryouts took stress to a new level. The drummers had to play that Haskell Harr standard, "The Downfall of Paris." (Maybe he *was* a Nazi doctor and the piece was triumphant—never occurred to me then.) For some reason I missed my scheduled appointment—why, I can't remember—and ended up playing it on my Haskell Harr book on the concrete bench under the pecan tree in front of the band room. Me and Mr. Goff. I remember him being in a good mood that day—which, given my less than astonishing playing, probably helped. Anyway, I was in—and as always with achieving a dream, the fleeting gratification gave way almost immediately to the weight of the new responsibilities.

Our class inaugurated the new high school in 1966-67, but the band room wasn't finished, so that fall we rehearsed in the old band room, then drove over to the practice field at the new school for marching. The five-minute drive accommodated the smokers perfectly. One afternoon we were driving over with senior drummer Steve Pitts; Bill French had prepared a cigarette for him—Pitts took it, it flopped limply with an obvious firecracker fuse hanging out the end. "Goddamn, French," said Pitts, matter of factly, tossing it and lighting another. He only had five minutes.

In August we went to band camp, over in Pine Mountain. It was here that we laid the foundation for the fall marching campaign, learned a lot of new music, and bonded as a group. We practiced marching twice a day, in the August sun. I don't remember a drop of rain ever at band camp. Our freshman year we were still playing pieces like "The Continental" and "Never on Sunday" in our halftime shows; that quickly graduated to "Alfie," "The Look of Love," "Yesterday," "The Fool on the Hill," "Eleanor Rigby," and "The Teaberry Shuffle," with dancing band—all Mr. Goff's arrangements and a different show every week. The first couple of years, 1966-67, we came on field with "Dixie Entry," a real crowd pleaser and Mr. Goff original that succumbed to the sensibility of the era. We worked hard. "Don't be alarmed by that wet stuff on your skin," Mr. Goff would say. "It's called sweat. It won't hurt you." And to anyone who considered wimpery in the face of a scolding: "That mean Mr. Goff! But that's okay, my mama loves me." A prime candidate for such a scolding would have been Milton Hutchinson, trombone, who just couldn't seem to get the marching-in-step business right. I can still hear Mr. Goff calling out the steps as we marched: "Left, right, Milton Hutchinson, left, right, Milton Hutchinson."

In the drummer cabin, Bill French, Kevin White, Mike Cadenhead, and I for some reason took our cots, folded the legs under them, laid them across the rafters, and slept up there. We always had illicit reading material in band camp. One year it was *My Secret Life* and *Naked Lunch*, the latter with its immortal sentence: "He grin and fart." You simply can't give sixteen-year-old boys a sentence like that. The book also introduced us to the word "rim" in a new context, and lent some spice to the "rim-tap" we did as the band filed somewhere. Once Mr. Goff counted off, "one-two-three-rim!" and we collapsed.

We also rehearsed in concert set-up under the pavilion—more chorales and more drummers fit for the devil's workshop. Mr. Goff had an amazing ear. I can picture his bit-into-a-lemon face as he heard something out of tune. He would wave the band dead, usually with an oblivious straggler playing an extra measure, drawing a frown (I learned the phrase "peripheral vision" from Mr. Goff), then point impatiently at the players in whatever section had offended, one by one, until he found the culprit, at which point he would writhe in his chair, grimace in agony, then bend the malefactor back into the natural world. I remember him teaching us about accent with the phrase "What is this thing called love?" *What?* Is this thing called love? What *is* this thing called love? What is this *thing* called love? What is this thing *called* love? What is this thing called—*love?* What is this thing called *love?*

Another feature of band camp was sectionals—which we of course called sexuals. The drummers went down to an amphitheater by the lake, where we enjoyed the immense good fortune of having the now-graduated Stonewall Breyer as our instructor. He would arrive at band camp in his little sports car with his full trap set, which he set up in his cabin. I could have stood there watching him play forever. Our job in sectionals was to learn the cadences, which we did with enormous pride. Some, like "Mambo," we inherited, others like "Talk, Talk" we made up, or one of us wrote, such as Rob Rainey's "Rob's Rim"—what else?—or Stonewall taught us—most memorably "7/8," which he adapted from Dave Brubeck's "Unsquare Dance" into very clever interlocking snare and tenor parts. It's hard to believe Mr. Goff let us use it; I guess it was just too rich, he couldn't resist it. He told the band just to block it out and keep marching left/right until it ended and something more sane, in four, returned. When we were freshmen, senior Bob Greenleaf (clarinet in concert season, an excellent musician) played bass drum in our corps; from tenth grade on, it was George Whelchel (string bass in concert season, also an excellent musician), whose approach to playing could only be called boogeying. We had soul. I just attended George's funeral last month. Shocking—a real loss. A kind and talented man. Everywhere we went we were a million times better than the other drummers—often girls with hair hanging down their backs—scandalous!—a prestige we enjoyed, and it's easy to see now we owed, at heart, to Mr. Goff.

One year at band camp things got a little rowdy one evening—marauding gangs of boys infiltrated the girls' areas, and I think water balloons may have been involved. When the chaperones finally reined in the chaos, one of them, Mr. Allison, a tall, wiry, generally very pleasant man who probably said two hundred words a year, was moved, given the extreme circumstances, to deliver a scolding that became legend. "I've got two daughters," he seethed. "One of them's away at school, the other one's here at band camp. Where's she at? I don't know where she's at! Has she been raped?" He let that sink in, then added, "All right, I'm going to bed. And if I have to get up for any reason at all—" He walked his menacing stare from one culprit to the next, waited, then concluded,

"*Look out.*" The number of dramatic performances of that speech, with lowered glasses and imaginary cigarette, is rivaled only by *Cats*.

Something else I remember about band camp—an important lesson learned. Wisely, we were granted plenty of recreation time, and toward the end of our stay we always had a skit night. In our skit one year a Nazi commander, sitting behind a desk, is waiting for the "important papers." People keep bringing the wrong thing and keep getting executed—by me, wearing somebody's purple plastic Nazi helmet, and gunning them down with a machine gun stick—sound effect provided by Bill French on a snare drum off-stage. Eventually somebody brings the "right" papers—toilet paper, and the commander rises in skivvies for a trip to the john. I achieved some celebrity as "Johnny Kraut," and I liked it so much I decided to reprise the character in a later, extemporized skit where it was no longer funny. The next year I remember Mr. Goff explaining to the new band members the desiderata of a good skit. He counseled against the ill-prepared and, yes, referenced a skit from the previous year which had gone on too long, with too little direction, and "just stunk." My face got hot. Mr. Goff richly appreciated creative humor, and was richly aware when those two qualities did not appear. When he said something stunk, you could pretty much go to the bank with it. No one ever had better taste or timing. (Bill remembers him tapping his foot in 4/4 while clapping a retarding pace with his hands. "It still mystifies me.") Important lesson: when something works, nail it, then leave it for good.

You can find pages of testimonials to Mr. Goff's greatness on Caring Bridge and elsewhere. I enjoy the communal gratification of reading those, but often feel something is left out. Most mention his character and influence and so forth, but few emphasize his personality. In other words, now that he's gone—and you have to endure the same thing at most funerals—the human being has been supplanted by his significance. In Mr. Goff's case, what gets left out is his defining trait: he was funny. Smart funny. He was never undignified, but he had a clownish side. Not that he laughed easily—you had to impress him, which was possible only if you were pulling your weight. There wasn't anything cheap about any of it. One of the great accomplishments of my life is that I could make Mr. Goff laugh. I've always been grateful that I have lived in a period of civilization where you didn't have to slay foes but could survive by being funny. Or die trying. I guess this has always been true for court fools, and I knew from a very early age that's basically what I was. If they don't laugh, I'm a goner—and all my life nothing has held more terror than the concept of being *not funny*. A couple of job interviews where my attempted jokes were met by Mt. Rushmore academics. Mrs. Taylor, English teacher, saying that's enough, you've gone too far, you're *not funny*, get out in the hall—and me going, okay, I'll be good—but too late. Mr. Elliot, assistant principal, calling me into his office to tell me in case I was wondering I was really just a pathetic weenie and *not funny*. Screw him. Making Mr. Goff laugh was worth something. Making anybody laugh, making *me* laugh, is worth something—and it's easy to see now that's what kept us going in those absurd adolescent years—or any years, come to think of it. I say "us" because the people who got me through high school, and that I helped get through high school, are easy to list now, and mostly *still* my friends. When I look back at the friendships of my life, the self-selected groups of kindred spirits, the obvious common denominator is laughter. If you want to understand people, follow the laughter. The point is, you could say Mr. Goff was exacting, demanding, an extremely effective teacher, with natural authority, and all the rest, and you wouldn't have him at all. That could be a lot of people. Mr. Goff was part of the laughter. Which gave you the sense that though he labored under some merciless genetic imperative, somewhere deeper he was wise to the grand comedy of it all. Mr. Goff had soul.

Which is why being on his bad side was just all-around not good, and a place you really didn't want to be.

I was a few times. A couple stand out.

One of Mr. Goff's rules was that when practice was done and you were walking from the field back to the band room, you could not play your instrument. This rule was very simple and very clear. The real point I'm after here concerns the mystery of the adolescent mind. One day I left practice pounding away on my drum. Don't ask me why—I can't tell you. Later, I was told that Mr. Goff had yelled at me to stop, several times, but I had just pounded obliviously away. The demerit I got was nothing compared to the cringing mental picture I subsequently had to entertain of Mr. Goff yelling at me, and me ignoring him. Then there was a memorable State Contest. The concert band went every spring to Tuscaloosa for State Contest. Three judges rated the band's performance, and another rated its ability in sight reading. The scores were 1—superior, 2—excellent, 3—good, 4—fair, 5—poor, and you ended up with four numbers, one from each judge. Needless to say, for our band, four 1's was the only acceptable score. Somewhere in the recent past a "2" lurked, like a shameful family secret, but otherwise it was all four 1s. Stories conflict slightly, but Mr. Goff's overall record in his thirty-two years at Auburn

High School was all 1s with, I'm pretty sure, two 2s. Anyway, this particular year, I have a mental picture of Mr. Goff running across the parking lot by the coliseum holding up four fingers. The ecstasy that accompanied this, regrettably, spilled over that evening, while he was out enjoying a celebratory dinner, into some skirmishes at the hotel with water balloons that rapidly escalated into a full-scale war with trash cans full of water being dumped on people in their rooms and that sort of thing. Mr. Goff was called away from his dinner, and I'll spare the hyperbole and just say he was *not happy*. I think the school had to pay the hotel damages. And we all got five demerits. But here's what my tired and mature mind can't fathom: *how could I have been so stupid?* And I'm not proud when I say there are a number of instances from that period of my life that demand an answer to that same question. Seems like I read somewhere that the synapses aren't fully formed yet or something in the adolescent brain. Must not be. I will say, I deal with adolescents myself today, and I cut them a lot of slack. They are different from you and me.

We knew that in most other places being in the band was pansy, but at Auburn High School being in the band was cool. One reason for that: Mr. Goff. He gave us the gift of prestige—but the *real* gift he gave all of us, of course, was *music*. Music is the greatest of the arts—it lives more fully apart from its notation—it shapes the mind like hands shape clay—it awakens vast and rich acreage of neural connections—it pierces the soul—it embodies memory. It doesn't indicate—it *is* emotion. You don't need any research to know that an engagement with the rhythm and melody and harmony of music leads to better brain function and a richer spiritual life. And they want to take it out of the schools? This is the fundamental problem of society: the poor in spirit make the rules. Enough. When I think of the music of my high school years, a number of memories flood in. I can still feel the auditorium on a balmy April supper concert night, filled with the lush strains of Leonard Bernstein—*West Side Story* overture, or the overture to *Candide*, the latter a blitzkrieg piece of music that should have been too much for us, but wasn't—still hear the call of the horns in the overture to *Lohengrin*. Ralph Vaughan Williams' *English Folk Song Suite*, Dvorak's *From the New World*, which (though composed by a little Czech man who loved trains) is itself about hope and promise and something already plaintive in the young soul of America, and was my doorway into the palace of romantic music. *Jubilee* march—I can still see Mr. Goff rocking back on the trio, for those few moments not conducting, but riding. The pride in his face. *American Overture*—in which I had a gong solo. Only one note, as gong solos tend to be. The gong doesn't exactly lend itself to paradiddles. But a very well-placed note. *Incantation and Dance*—a percussion orgy, requiring a homemade slapstick made out of 1x4's. And a ton more. It seems as though music is the one thing that time can't erase. The people, the places, the eras fade—and what's left?—the *music*—the only way, except for certain smells, you can access the past anymore, which has been reduced to a series of musical stepping stones through the dissipating vapor trail of time. Clearly, the entire human story will resolve itself, when this world is an ember, to our particular symphony—which you will catch strains of as you cruise past this vacant lot of the galaxy. I didn't come from a particularly musical family—I wouldn't have had any of this without Mr. Goff. Everything I know about music, which admittedly isn't much, I owe to him. That I, a moderately talented small-town nobody, could be a part of something like this was, after all my parents gave me, probably the greatest gift of my life. And then there were the genuinely talented. I think what Mr. Goff was proudest of was the best among us (he always found them, or they him) who went on to be real musicians after high school—and there were many.

He was a much more complicated man than I understood at the time. One of the feelings I remember most vividly about being in the band was the seriousness that came over us as we neared District or State Contest. The levity shriveled, replaced by a universal concentration of body mind and soul no longer just on the pieces themselves, but on nuance, dynamics, finesse. Polish. You could see it in everybody's face. Every ounce of everyone's energy was concentrated on the performance. If you were given a choice between committing Hari Kari and letting Mr. Goff down—go ahead and get the sword. We entered the Zone, where the whole was so much greater than the sum of the parts, what came over us was and still is a mystery. Mr. Goff's personality combined musicianship, discipline, humor, passion, and class—amazingly, this also describes the band.

How he infused himself into our corps, I have no idea, but something tells me it is the secret of greatness. And it was only later that I understood what it cost him. Another key part of Mr. Goff's make-up, which he did *not* infuse into the band, was a close to debilitating anxiety which I learned about later—but I do know that, difficult as it is to achieve excellence, it is far more difficult to keep it. Yes, everyone's expectations become unsparingly distorted—but that's nothing compared to your own. The pressure on him, within him, was immense. I guess the surprise in all this was the revelation that Mr. Goff had his own life. Apart from us, Mr. Goff's instrument was the trumpet—I can still see it standing alone at his funeral in October 2008—and we vaguely knew he played jazz gigs—also string bass—somewhere occasionally on weekends—he loved Count Basie!—and had been a part of the Auburn Knights, the fabled AU dance band—but all of that was peripheral when we knew him. I don't remember ever hearing him *play* the trumpet, except for training purposes, which he could do on any instrument, if a little spastic on drums. Bill French did hear him play once, and tells this story: "Once after school I had to go back to the band room. He was in the room with the electronic tuners playing trumpet. It was stunning. He stopped playing as if I had walked in on something. Since that afternoon I think of him as a refugee from big bands, no place to play and mouths to feed. I heard Ira Sullivan in a Fort Lauderdale club last year—his tone was the same as Mr. Goff." That story, which I only recently heard, suggests another dimension to the man—the musician who might have been in some hot orchestra, a stand-out, composer, arranger, conductor, perhaps, but who became a high school band director (the reasons his business), and knew that his salvation lay in doing it superlatively. Talk about stress. I look back through my memories and I don't really see that. A private thing that you couldn't really know. I just see a funny, extremely effective man. That appearance now too seems a herculean effort of his. It was his humor, or his soul, however you want to phrase it. And then there was Mrs. Goff—a beautiful lady just out of the spotlight. She died a year and a half before him, which basically finished him. I had not realized at the time the depth of their bond.

He never made much money. They lived in a small house, he drove a crummy car. After their children got older, Mrs. Goff was able to work and contribute. Funny, I saw him only three or four times after high school. You think things will stay the same—I'll come visit, we'll stay in touch, etc.—but time doesn't really permit this. My own students today say this—after I've come to know them for four years, and the end comes—they'll stay in touch, they'll write, they'll visit—but I know better. When an era passes, it's gone. That's what makes it an era. For three years the last gig of the year was playing *Pomp and Circumstance* at graduation—then, weirdly enough, they're playing it for you. Mr. Goff suffered a serious stroke in 1989, and retired. He recovered so well he later said he had walked away too soon. He went on to direct the band at a private school, and give private lessons. But, sadly—beyond sadly—the stroke had robbed him of his ability to play. In the '90s he and Mrs. Goff came to one of mine and Ken Clark's musical comedies in Columbus, and I've never been more nervous in my life. He was still funny (not sure if *we* were), with white hair. It was the last time I ever saw him.

I think the success of a society depends on people like Mr. Goff—identifying them and making sure they're in position to do what they do unsabotaged by the moronic rules of people not like Mr. Goff. When I think of the billions of dollars wasted trying to cram the circle of education into the square of bureaucratic control, I'm sad, knowing it will always be so—but encouraged, knowing that the Mr. Goffs of this world will always transcend that crap. Mr. Goff, motivated by something within himself, took the sons and daughters of the professors and tradesmen of a small college town and fashioned them into a great band, allowing them to experience the process, at a young age, of achieving something excellent. The paradigm became imprinted. I see a reflection of the same experience in the eyes and hear it in the voices of some of my own students sometimes, who played on a sports team, perhaps, that won a state championship—that experience of having lost themselves in a *team*, of having risen above their own egos, and accomplished something extraordinary. What better than this can you give a young person?

Ego, along with muscle tone and short term memory, melts anyway. You cease being yourself and become what you have created and loved. As Auden said of Yeats—"he became his admirers"—so Mr. Goff has become the self he gave away.

Mr. Goff, circa 1970s

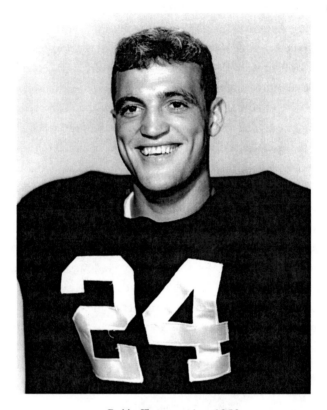

Bobby Freeman, circa 1953

Photographs courtesy of Auburn University Library
Special Collections and Archives Department

Time and Bobby Freeman
May 21, 2014

I haven't exactly been an avid watcher of Super Bowls. But I did make it through some of this year's, and thought I saw clearly one phase of football giving way to another. Maybe Denver just had a bad game, but those two teams play five times, I don't like Denver's chances in any of the five. Peyton Manning, in the right landscape, was a good quarterback. He hasn't changed, but the landscape has: Some new element has come into the game. The athleticism—the pace and nature of the game—have jumped to a higher level, college and pro. Football evolves like everything else. When everybody gets used to doing something one way, the advantage belongs to whoever can get outside it—like the genius who first decided to throw that fat rugby ball over the cloud of dust a hundred years ago. After this latest no-contest mercifully ended, I found myself thinking about Bobby Freeman.

In the eighties I ran a small printing shop in Auburn. I had been away for some years, and come back. I breathed and dreamed that business for five years, living in various places in and around town where I did little more than sleep. Among other spots I spent some time in an old house in Notasulga, then for a while rented a little house across from the War Eagle Supper Club. The neighbors were rowdy and my landlord was Bobby Freeman.

I had heard of him but didn't really know much about him. But during that period I came to know him, and used to enjoy going by his real estate office, where kicked back behind his desk he would give you the impression he had all day to talk to you. He had been in school in Auburn in the early fifties, and I always like talking to people who were in my place before me. It's like a taste of nirvana to hear about your formative landscape minus you—all the stress and toil, you yourself cool as a cucumber in your non-existence—not quite the same, but kin, to imagining your absence from the place after you leave. Mr. Freeman still displaced a good bit of the atmosphere, and it was easy to sense the athlete, even the badass, he had been. But he was in his fifties at that point and all that had fallen away, dissolved by time. He considered his own past self with amused detachment, and his thoughts were clearly tending to the non-material. He didn't talk about his football career unless you asked him.

One of the reasons I went into the printing business was to start a magazine. However one does that—I still don't have a clue. But of course I immediately found myself maxed out by the relentless demands of a small business, and it took me probably two years even to make a first attempt. I managed three or four amateurish little eight-pagers. I wrote some short pieces for them, then wrote some other pieces that are still waiting, forlornly—conceived but undelivered. Among the latter was an interview with Bobby Freeman—which my post-Super Bowl train of thought led me to go dig up.

A great Yeats line (among many) I can't seem to forget is, "Who could have foretold that the heart grows old?" Getting up in years, I'm learning, is disconcerting in ways you could never have understood or predicted when young. The same holds true for the consolations. Seeing the transience of everything from a higher vantage point turns out to be strangely restful, though the price is an acceptance of one's own transience and the vanity of all things. After a few decades have come and gone, you've seen so many arcs in your life, you see the arc of everything. Whatever you see, you don't see just as it "is," but also as it must have been and will likely become. Experience in life changes points to line segments. The mental photography becomes time-lapse, and the present tense turns just like muscle to fat. The center cannot hold.

Mr. Freeman died in 2003, another gulf of time after that interview in the eighties, a gulf of time itself beyond his playing days some twenty-five years before that.

They called him the "Goose"—for his brash and reckless approach to the game, and you could still see it in his eyes. He played at Auburn from 1951 to 1954, and went on to a professional career that lasted until 1962. A photographic collage from the 1954 Gator Bowl victory over Baylor, a few other plaques and pictures, dotted the walls of his office, and he laughed as I told him I wanted to hear about his past. "Yes, I'm a relic of a by-gone era," he said, "like the old neighborhood grocery store and candy-striped barber poles."

He was born in Birmingham in 1932, and his father moved his family to Decatur in 1938. He grew up there, but spent most of his youth on his grandparents' farm in Walker County. "We didn't know the word 'Depression' then. We never went without anything, and if we were poor we didn't know it." He loved listening to the radio (*The Shadow, The Green Hornet, The Lone Ranger*), followed Alabama football and the exploits of Harry Gilmer, and the Brooklyn Dodgers. His earliest ambition was to play professional baseball. He remembered the attack on Pearl Harbor when he was nine, and his family following the reports of Walter Winchell and Gabriel Heatter throughout the war.

Not surprisingly, he was athletically precocious and played everything in high school. He was quick to tell you that one of the most important influences in his life was his high school football coach, the legendary H. L. "Shorty" Ogle, now in the Alabama Sports Hall of Fame. Ogle was the first of many legendary coaches Freeman played for, who invented and patented a one-piece elastic corset-pad ("bloomer pads"), integrated the now-common check-off system into signal-calling, and was the first coach in Alabama to use the T-formation. He was also a strict disciplinarian. "Like all young people I was strong-willed and thought I knew everything. I needed his authority."

A quarterback and defensive back, Freeman was the best athlete in his town, a local celebrity, the subject of many articles, and the recipient of many unofficial bonuses such as a milk shake from a particular druggist for each touchdown he scored, usually four or five a week. As he neared graduation, Ogle took him aside and told him he had a chance to play college ball and get an education. Oddly enough, those two ideas used to go together. In the East-West All-Star baseball game that year, 1949, in Birmingham, Freeman was voted Most Valuable Player, and remembered vividly the two solid hits he got that night. The St. Louis Cardinals offered him a baseball contract, but he had been visiting the campuses of Georgia Tech, Mississippi State, Alabama, and Auburn, and mainly because he had been impressed with the people, he had already accepted a football scholarship to Auburn.

"When I was young," he remembered, "I was not a respecter of others. I saw the world through the first-person singular. I thought I knew a lot more than I did. Playing football at Auburn was an enlightening experience for me. I was used to being the King Bee, and all of a sudden I had to prove myself all over again."

The spring of 1951 happened to be the freshman spring of another of the instrumental figures in Freeman's life, Coach Ralph "Shug" Jordan. On the surface it may have seemed an inauspicious time to begin a football career at Auburn. The Tigers had hardly been a powerhouse the past few years under Coach Earl Brown: five straight losing seasons, the last, 1950, still the worst year in Auburn football history, an 0-10 campaign with seven shutouts. Frustration reigned; morale sank to the basement. Coach Jordan had played at Auburn himself from 1928-1932, and had sixteen years of SEC coaching experience when he signed a five-year contract with Auburn in February of 1951. He had spent his last five years under Wally Butts at Georgia. "Coach Jordan was a product of the Wally Butts' school—hard-nosed, tough, physical football with no shortcuts. His philosophy was 'if you whip the guy in front of you, not too much bad can happen,' and I guess that's still pretty much true today. He worked us so hard I thought sometimes I was going to die. We would practice till dark, and there were some nights I was so tired I would forgo supper. And I've got to be *tired* to forgo supper."

End of one era, beginning of another.

"Coach Jordan was an Irish Catholic from Selma who had tremendous qualities of leadership. Psychologically, he could put you where he wanted you. He believed in hard work—he always said there's more character in a bead of sweat than anything else—but he knew when to let up, when to call the team together for a talk. He ruled out of both respect and fear. But his real strength was his mental control of his team. He was a psychological master."

Freeman admitted he was "rambunctious and wild," but Shug recognized his ability early and gave him an opportunity to develop it. Freshmen were eligible to play in the early fifties, and Freeman averaged thirty-eight minutes a game his first year, playing both offensive and defensive halfback. The first time he got the ball, in a game against Wofford College at Cramton Bowl in Montgomery, he ran a seventy-nine-yard touchdown. "That told me I could do it."

In the Georgia game that year, in six-degree weather at Columbus, Freeman got a lick he still vividly remembered. A forearm to the jaw from Marion Campbell, which knocked out his two front teeth. "It neutralized me," he laughed. Dazed, he looked around on the ground for his teeth, thinking maybe he'd put them back in. He shook it off, played the rest of the game, and a dentist later pulled out the stubs. A few years down the road, when they were both playing professionally, Freeman confronted Campbell. "I told him, 'you don't remember this, but you knocked my two front teeth out.' He said it looked like I had survived it, so I must be a good man."

Auburn went 5-5. Then came Freeman's sophomore year, his personal low point, and a disappointing year for the team. Playing quarterback, Freeman broke his wrist early in the fall and sat out the rest of the year. The team went 2-8. Watching helplessly from the sidelines, Freeman felt like a misfit with his injury. I asked him if he ever thought of, you know . . . "Leaving? Shoot, there were times when I had my bags packed." (Like Bo, getting on that bus back to Bessemer and his mama his freshman year.) Freeman's high school sweetheart, who became his wife and business partner, Rita, was at Florence State Teacher's College. Being away from her, and from his family, was killing him. He used to hitchhike home to see them. Also, he had a brother playing at Navy, and during this year gave serious thought to transferring there. But he survived the gloom and frustration and remained at Auburn—fortunately, since his last two years were outstanding.

1953—Freeman's junior year—Coach Jordan installed the famous X and Y team system, alternating Vince Dooley (X) and Freeman (Y) at quarterback. Dooley ran the more conventional offense, and the "Goose" directed a more wide-open approach. "You've got the goal line down there a certain distance away, and your job is to get there, however you can do it. You can go a few yards at a time, or you can go in a hurry. Either way. I liked to run the ball, or maybe throw it down there to Jim Pyburn, whatever it took." In the Georgia game, which Auburn won for the first time since 1942, Freeman had a ninety-five-yard punt return for a touchdown, still an Auburn record, "mainly because nobody is dumb enough to catch a punt on the five-yard line." Down the Georgia sideline he streaked, Wally Butts cursing him angrily all the way. Auburn finished the season with its best record since 1935, 7-2-1. The team set fourteen new team and individual records, and Jordan was named SEC Coach of the Year. The Tigers went to the Gator Bowl, January 1, 1954, but lost to Texas Tech in what proved to be the breakthrough game in Red Raider football history (the victory over Baylor commemorated on Freeman's office plaque was also played in 1954, on December 31, but following the next season.)

Freeman led the SEC in total offense his senior year. Dooley had graduated, and the X and Y system slowly petered out during the season. Auburn won eight and lost three that year, beating Alabama for the first time since 1949. That game, a 28-0 shutout, was one of Freeman's best games at Auburn. He led Auburn to their first touchdown, scored the second on a forty-one-yard option run, led them on their third drive, and scored the last touchdown on a quarterback sneak, which had been set up by two long passes. The 33-13 victory over Baylor in the Gator Bowl featured the "run of the year," a forty-three-yard scamper by future governor Fob James. When Freeman graduated, he left a program he had helped get back on its feet. The remainder of the fifties and the early sixties would be one of the greatest eras at Auburn. (Followed by one of the worst—as Bear Bryant and Alabama took the game out of the fifties to a level of athleticism and strategy that dominated Auburn—and most everybody else—until Pat Sullivan arrived in 1969, then dominated them for another decade after he left. And I don't recall anyone attempting to change the rules to prevent it.)

"Some of the greatest moments in football are not reflected on the scoreboard. You make a lot of friends, and you learn the joy of playing together as a team. You learn the importance of execution, the mental aspects of the game. Whenever you learn something, you learn it as a team; everybody has a part in it. I never read the papers much. It doesn't matter what anybody thinks but your teammates. You can't fool them. If you aren't pulling your weight, they know it. The main thing is, we had fun playing college ball. Coach Jordan wanted you to have fun. Football without fun is just monotonous. Coach Jordan's philosophy was 'you can't succeed at anything without enthusiasm.' It catches and works its way down through everybody involved. I like to think the kids today have as much fun, but college football today is big business; it's paying big bills. There's a lot more stress involved. The kids today are bigger and stronger and more specialized. But I was never one for weights. My roommate in college used to lift weights, and I'd come in at night and trip over them and get mad at him. Good athletes will fool you. Strength manifests itself in a lot of different ways. It's not necessarily muscle and bulk. Some of the best athletes I ever knew were the kind of guys you could be in a room with and never know they were athletes. If they were in a Charles Atlas ad, they'd be the 'before.' A good athlete must have coordination and rhythm and what we used to call 'country tough.' And at a certain point, instinct takes over. I think some guys build themselves up more for the mirror than anything else. That's not it at all."

In January of 1955, Bobby Freeman, guard George Atkins, and Jack Locklear (center, linebacker whom Freeman considered the best all-around athlete ever to play at Auburn) went to Mobile for the Senior Bowl. Freeman was named Most Valuable Player in the game, and won a Rolex watch. After the game, Coach Al Sherman signed him to a no-cut contract with the Winnipeg Blue Bombers of the Canadian Football League. Shortly after that, however, he was drafted in the third round of the NFL draft by the Cleveland Browns. Paul Brown, owner and head coach of the team, called him and explained that he needed him in Cleveland. Freeman told him about the contract he had already signed, but Brown dismissed that, insisting that these kinds of contracts were broken all the time. So Bob and Rita (who had gotten married after his junior year) went to Cleveland. They hadn't been there long, however, when Al Sherman appeared and had Freeman subpoenaed into court where the judge ruled he couldn't play ball professionally in the United States for two years. Rather than tie up his career in Canada, Freeman decided to join the Army, where he played service ball for two seasons with the 101st Airborne, stationed in Fort Jackson, South Carolina. When he had served his time, he took his family back to Cleveland to begin his professional career in the 1957 season.

The Browns were a power at that time. They won their division almost every year. Otto Graham had recently retired, and George Ratterman was the quarterback. Jim Brown was a rookie. ("He was a fine, fine athlete—about 6'3", 220, and he could run like a deer. He had the great ability of never letting you get a clear shot at him.") Freeman came on as a defensive back, and would face such receivers as Harlon Hill, Dave Middleton, Red Phillips, Lenny Moore, Raymond Berry, and Bobby Mitchell. He also held for placekicker Lou Groza. After his first couple of years, Jim Brown got his salary up around $25,000, making him and Paul Hornung the highest paid players in the league, but salaries in the $8,000-$10,000 range were the rule. There were plenty of All-Pro linemen earning $9,500. Freeman started out at $14,000—"and that was a lot of money then." The Freemans, with three children, would live in Cleveland for six months, then bring a nice sum home to Alabama in the off-season. Those were the days when many players thought of pro football as a way of making a little money for a few years before finding a job. Freeman was making good money, but the adjustment he had had to make to the higher level of talent around him in college hardly compared to the adjustment he now had to make. "Everybody up there is good—it's just a question of how good. The competition is unbelievable, and it's a different kind of competition than college and high school—you're competing for your livelihood. You've got to believe in yourself, because there's always going to be somebody telling you you aren't good enough—probably the guy who wants your job. In the pros you've got to develop finesse—develop your skills to a very high degree to have a chance. And you've got to play hurt, because everybody is hurt. You play with injuries you wouldn't think about playing with in college."

The Browns were a highly sophisticated organization. "Paul Brown was a genius. He was a great believer in the mental aspects of the game. The first thing he did in camp was give you an IQ test. He made you write down what every player did on every play, and you left camp with a notebook full. All his assistant coaches were intellectual kind of people. Paul (most coaches in the NFL wanted their players to call them by their first names) owned the ball club and was the head coach, and called all the plays." The Browns lost the championship game to Detroit in 1957, and in 1958 were beaten out by the Giants in six inches of snow, in the last game of the regular season, on a forty-nine-yard Pat Summerall field goal.

After two seasons, Freeman went over to Green Bay in a trade that included Willie Davis, Henry Jordan, and Lou Carpenter. That was Vince Lombardi's first year with the Packers, and he faced a task similar to the one that had faced Shug

Jordan at Auburn in 1951, and he went about it in a similar way. "Coach Lombardi (no 'Vinny' here) was a very stern disciplinarian who was great to his players as long as they did what they were supposed to. They respected him because he knew the game and he was a great teacher. He ruled by the fine. He felt that the most effective way to get results with professional people was through their pocketbooks. He'd fine you for being late to a meeting, and being late meant not being there five minutes early." What were the reasons for his success? "His intensity, his desire for everyone around him to excel. He surrounded himself with good people, like Phil Bengston the defensive coach, and he had the philosophy that if you were in better physical condition than the other guy, when it got right down to it, you'd win out."

Freeman spent one year with the Packers—a team which with a strong defense built around Ray Nitschke, the great offensive line of Jim Ringo, Fuzzy Thurston, Jerry Kramer, and Forrest Gregg, receivers Max McGee and Boyd Dowler, runners Paul Hornung and Jim Taylor, and, not least, quarterback Bart Starr—was on the threshold of becoming one of the great dynasties in the history of the league. Starr, with the help of a great teacher who nurtured his confidence, and his own strong personal discipline, "made himself into a great football player."

"Some athletes," Freeman told me, "have only average ability and have to work a lot harder and have a lot more determination and tenacity. The best athletes are generally lazy. They rely on their ability and do just what they have to do. It comes easy for them. I'll tell you one thing—you may not win a Kentucky Derby with plugs, but the guy with average ability and a lot of heart—it's not always true—but he's the guy you can usually count on, you know what I mean?" Green Bay finished in third place that year, remarkable for a perennial cellar-dweller.

In 1960, Freeman was traded to the Philadelphia Eagles, who beat the Packers for the league championship that year. Norm van Brocklin was the quarterback, and Sonny Jurgensen was the back-up. Freeman remembered Van Brocklin for his "mental tenacity" as well as his great ability. Jurgensen, who would later go to the Redskins and a brilliant career, was "possibly the greatest of them all." In his second year at Philadelphia, the Eagles lost the title game to the Giants. That was the year Frank Gifford received the vicious hit from Chuck Bednarik that would knock him unconscious for two days, and keep him out of football for a year and a half, and after which he would never be the same. Freeman, pursuing a few yards away on that play, never forgot it.

Freeman played his last year in the NFL in 1962 with the Redskins. They finished in third place. At the end of the season, he asked Coach McPeak for a raise, but was told there would be no raises that year. He made the decision to retire. "I was not hurt, and the gray matter hadn't trickled out of my ears yet. I was about thirty-one years old, and I could have played a few more years, but I had kids I had to pull out of school every six months, and I had drug Rita all over the United States. We decided to come back home."

A memorable career. What did he gain from it? "I guess the main thing is humility. Everybody in the NFL is equal, and you're just a speck in the sand. It made me realize that this country is a melting pot—you play with people of all backgrounds and nationalities. You learn that they bleed red just like you. You drop some of your small southern town feelings, because you can't help but respect great athletic talent wherever you see it. And perseverance. You get knocked down in the trenches and you get back up, your eyes black and your lips bloody, and you try again. You can't ever give up. You know what they say: 'the big coon walks right before dawn'."

The Freemans came home to Decatur, and Bob worked for a couple of years with a construction firm there before returning to football as an assistant coach at Auburn under Coach Jordan. He came the year after Jimmy Sidle and Tucker Frederickson graduated, 1964, and coached through the sixties, and the Sullivan-Beasley era, until 1973, the year after the Amazins'. Then, with the help of Jack Shannon, he got involved in real estate, and he and Rita became prominent realtors in Auburn.

"Rita's my guiding light. We have been blessed in a lot of ways. If we ever needed money, it seems like it just came. But I don't think about material things as much as I used to. As you grow older, I think it's a natural progression, you think more of the spiritual. I think you need strong convictions in your life. Serve the Lord the best you can, fire both barrels, and leave the world a better place. That's my cracker barrel philosophy. Athletics have been good to me. I had my day in the sun, and I wouldn't trade my experience for anything. But if you dwell on the past, you are the past."

I sold Village Printers in 1986—it became Tiger Prints, Ink, and, I think, has since changed hands a few times. It's still there—on College Street.

But a lot else is not.

As a kid delivering papers in the early sixties, I used to ride up to town on my bike on South Gay Street, at that time a graceful, oak-shaded street lined with beautiful old houses. Graceful and beautiful have become tacky and ugly, and whoever let the Snopeses rape that street, and a great deal else of Auburn, should be, but of course aren't, serving prison time. Too much past has been traded for too little present. I haven't lived in Auburn for twenty-five years. My parents are both gone—it's not my town anymore, though I still know a lot of people and have many good friends there. Still, I can't bring myself even to drive down Brookside Drive where I grew up. Strangers living in our house? All I can do with that is try not to think about it. The building that housed my print shop, on Bragg Avenue, has been remodeled (beautifully) into a residence, but the magazine dreams, along with most others, are long extinct. The house in Notasulga burned down years ago—haven't been able to drive by there either. Doc Markle's estate out Highway 29 where I spent several good years in a little cabin, is long since sold, parceled up, and barely recognizable, a little house I lived in on Dean Road, and the house across from the War Eagle Supper Club (where my dog Georgia once inexplicably squatted over the feet of visiting landlady Rita Freeman, and peed on her stylish shoes. It was—awkward), are both long gone—I mean physically gone—and the worst of it is, there is still, in 2014, nothing there. Only vacant derelict lots. Whatever Auburn is now, and the good heart of it does remain, despite my laments, no longer belongs to me, and has made very clear it has no further need of me, as time, in its patient but inexorable way, systematically erases my traces.

It's all very poetic.

Faulkner said, "It is my ambition to be, as a private individual, abolished and voided from history."

I know what he meant.

Auburn, 1951
(I don't know the woman in the photograph. I just like the photo!)

George Alfonso Wright, circa 1969

Photograph courtesy of Auburn University Library
Special Collections and Archives Department

George Alfonso Wright

July 2015

The first time I saw George Alfonso Wright he gave me a serious start. This would have been in the mid-eighties when he, born in 1899, was in his. At that time I was in the throes of the printing business, in my shop on Bragg Avenue in Auburn. One day I became suddenly aware of a figure standing at the open back door, like a sudden cut in a horror movie. He hadn't come—he was just *there*. I jumped.

Where had he come from so stealthily, without warning? And such an odd-looking figure, suggesting, perhaps, an elderly and inquisitive penguin—not a large man, bent with age, propped on a cane, pants belted just under his ribcage, his eyes shielded like a nuclear reactor technician's and his head tilted back in the attitude of the blind—which I was soon to discover he almost was. He still had a little sight in one eye, enough to allow him to navigate his way around the block from his duplex somewhere nearby, on his afternoon constitutional. Around his neck on a black ribbon hung an odd little magnifying glass.

He said he was curious about the goings-on here, and apologized for the intrusion—I assured him it was quite all right. The printing business ruled my life then and kept the stress level on extra-high—and I'll be honest, I secretly appreciated the occasional diversion. I walked over, we introduced ourselves, and from there developed a friendship that lasted until his death in 1992.

Mr. Wright enjoyed talking—with an acute, thoughtful, no doubt some would say maddening precision—and, as I learned over the next few years, he had a lot to say. True, his appearances in the shop weren't always well-timed—he used to annoy particularly my pressman, George—but I always found time to talk to him. Middle-aged people are busy. Busy busy busy. My mother used to hate that word, and I'm only now, with age, beginning to fully appreciate its tiresomeness myself. But when you *are* middle-aged, and the economic dimension of life is exaggerated at the expense of the others, you are holding up the world, and can be excused. People in their eighties are *remembering* the world, and have generally lost their taste for excuses.

In Mr. Wright's case—*really* remembering it.

He was what I would call a Rememberer.

* * *

I recently retired—a milestone followed closely by the destruction of my backyard office by a suicidal hickory tree—and I was suddenly confronted by the contents of two rooms that had become catchbasins for about thirty and twenty years of the detritus of my life, respectively. What to do? I thought about two things in making this decision. The first was the ordeal—it might have been Hercules' thirteenth labor—of clearing out my parents' house after Mama moved out. People save everything, time passes, somebody else throws it away. That's the way of the world. The second concerned my handling of mail—back when it was a viable form of communication. For me, all mail fell into one of three categories. The first, and smallest by far: mail that actually mattered—i.e., mostly bills. The second, bigger: obvious junk mail, which went straight into the trash. The third, biggest of all: everything else. This ambivalent matter I put into a box for future reference that never, ever came; and then about once a year I would throw it all away, and start over. So, as I looked at the two mountains of *stuff*, I thought of the love I bore my children and—you guessed it, the packrat in me lost its case, and I dumped everything. It was an unexpectedly liberating and cleansing feeling.

When I went to the Auburn University library to do a little research on Mr. Wright for this piece, the helpful archivists had to wheel out the boxes on a rolling table. Entire files of his correspondence, dating to 1902—letters to and from everybody under the sun—family members, friends, celebrities. Decades of receipts, all of his schoolwork, programs of events dating back to the teens, programs of class reunions over the years, *thousands* of photographs and negatives, with detailed, handwritten indexes. And this was only what he had donated to the university! It was clear that Mr. Wright, who graduated from Alabama Polytechnic Institute (as it was then called) in 1919 in Electrical Engineering, had thrown away nothing.

And, having known him, I would have expected exactly that.

He was a Rememberer.

* * *

As I grew up in Auburn in the '50s and '60s, first on Woodfield, later on Brookside, the town was oriented south to north in my inner cartography, centering on the arteries of Gay Street and Wrights Mill Road. Especially Wrights Mill. That's the way I rode my bike to school at Samford Avenue, or to town. There's no telling how many times I pumped up that incline, pre-dawn on

Sunday mornings to the *Birmingham News* office, aiming toward the three windows of the house at the end on Samford, still there, looking obliviously contemporary—don't those windows know their place in my mythology? Or, south, to Wrights Mill Road School, where I attended fifth and sixth grades, or farther, to Chewacla—a hot-spot swimming lake in those days. I can also remember some Boy Scout hikes out Wrights Mill—and, later, driving Mary Cobb home, shocking her by inviting her to sit in the front seat (she declined). Mary ironed for Mama on Fridays, and had occasionally babysat us when we were little. She was one of the sweetest people I ever knew, who some years later killed her husband. I grew up so accustomed to the words "Wrights Mill" I didn't really consider their meaning until probably my teen years. Oh, it was a *mill*. And it was *Wright's*. And I admit, it wasn't right away either that I understood it had been located in what is now Chewacla State Park, at the terminus of Wrights Mill Road.

So when Mr. Wright told me, early in our acquaintanceship, that he was of *that* Wright family, I listened with interest.

* * *

At first, our visits all took place in my printing shop, where they were footnotes to the activity of that frenetic business. I listened raptly, but recorded little, and so I'm left now with only my poor memory and a page or two of notes (and those archive boxes), and the realization that my values have exactly reversed. His was the real story, the letterheads and brochures the footnote. But I was busy busy busy. Same thing with my great-grandmother, Miss Ola Davis, born in the 1870s, who lived to be 106, and to whom I listened as a boy—alas, unretentively.

But as I said, "Wrights Mill" caught my ear.

W. W. (William Wilmot) Wright, Alfonso's (there were so many Georges around they had to go by middle names) grandfather, was born in 1825. I didn't find much about the family before the Civil War, but after it they were well established in Lee County and showing some industry. W. W. Wright acquired the mill that took on his name about 1873. Actually, there were two mills: one that ground corn and wheat, and the Gin-Saw Hole, a water-powered gin and sawmill. Those mills date to the 1840s, long before the current lake was created, though another dam was in place at that time, with the grist mill just below it on the west bank of Moore's Creek. The Gin-Saw Hole sat just before the spot where Town Creek, which more or less follows Wrights Mill Road from town to Chewacla, flows into Chewacla Creek in the three-creeked park. Back then too, the place was a popular swimming hole. The ownership of the mill before 1873 is convoluted and tedious, but after acquiring the grist mill, W. W. Wright operated it into the early years of the twentieth century, his miller for most of those years a certain Joe Broome, then gave it up and moved to town. So Alfonso had no real memory of it in operation.

For the last third of the nineteenth century, and the first third of the twentieth, as Auburn and the school it hosted steadily grew, the Wrights Mill area remained a popular recreation spot five miles south of town that attracted swimmers, hikers, bikers, and picnickers. In the early 1890s a clubhouse was built on the hill between the two mills, much frequented by townies, that is, until the sewage of the steadily growing town robbed Town Creek of its charm. I can remember sewage in that creek as a boy, but let's not dwell on that. Around 1900, a bicycle club was formed, and the members constructed a bicycle path from town out to the area, beginning at the south edge of town—i.e., where Gay Street terminated at Samford Avenue, and following the east bank of Town Creek for most of the way. B. B. Ross and the indefatigable Dr. George Petrie (among other things, author of the Auburn Creed) were key members.

Today in Chewacla State Park a bluff overlooks a dramatic gorge, and it was from there that the young star-crossed Creek warrior Chewacla, and his beloved, also unfortunately his cousin, in what is apparently a universal story, plunged hand in hand. Various versions of this story exist, but Mollie Hollifield, a remarkable woman, among the earliest Auburn coeds, and early Auburn historian, in the chapter "The Legend of Chewakla" in her 1955 book *Auburn: Loveliest Village of the Plain*, offers an appropriately floral rendition. They met on the fateful day—he with "a panther's grace," she "like a poised and lovely dryad of the forest." His father, the Chief, had forbidden the match and, we are told, despite all pleas was as adamant as an oak. By the 1930s the name "Chewacla" was inseparable from the area, so the Depression-era project became Chewacla State Park in 1939. Future state representative Pete Turnham came as an early teen to work with the CCC in the construction of the lake and park, and after serving in the Army during the war, came back to Auburn. He served forty-four years in the Alabama House of Representatives, still a record.

* * *

Mr. Wright would appear in the doorway, pressman George would roll his eyes, and I would go over to greet him. How was he today? "Middling, for an old blind man." His prodigious memory had but one weakness (one that is, I believe, common to us all): his remembering what he had already told you. Over the years of our friendship it became, let's just say, *well established* that he grew up in a house on what is now Opelika Road, graduated from API in 1919, spent thirty-five years with GE in Indianapolis, his cousin Clark Hudson had been president of Auburn National Bank, and he had made some mistakes in his life "when my hindsight was better than my foresight by a durn sight."

He always had something specific to share. One afternoon he came in and was curious if I happened to know how large the federal deficit was. I didn't know, but learned that it was a trillion dollars. Did I have any grasp of the magnitude of a trillion dollars? As chance would have it, I didn't. "Imagine someone sitting in a chair before a table counting one dollar a second." He licked a finger and provided a dramatic enactment. "He doesn't stop to eat, doesn't take a leak, just keeps counting, one dollar a second, and when the dollar bills pile up too high somebody comes and takes them away and keeps bringing in a new supply. How long do you think it would take him to count a trillion dollars?"

Tell me.

"Thirty-one thousand, six hundred and eighty-eight point aught seven years."

What did I think of *that*?

I was impressed. But what really impressed me, as I got to know him over the years, and what I liked about him, was that he wasn't really motivated by ego or self-interest. What he craved was accuracy. Only when he had no choice would he resort to a "horseback figure."

My own memory is impressionistic—centered on imagistic residue and feeling; his was centered on facts. When I tell a story from the past, I might frame it with "I was in the third grade or something." He framed his with, "I remember it was nineteen aught nine, a Tuesday, about 11:20, 11:30, and it had been raining that day . . ."

How did he do that?

Another day he came in and handed me a notecard with the following typed passage:

> "Finished files are the result of years of scientific study combined with the experience of years."

He asked me how many times the letter "f" appeared in it. I made a quick count, and I guess said "three." "When did you last have your eyes checked?" he asked me. Like most people on a first glance, I had omitted the "ofs." Why? Maybe because the reading eye moves from substance to substance, trained to deduce, not see, prepositions. The answer is six. He explained that this was one of his many icebreakers on a sales call.

One Christmas in that period I had gotten my father a copy of Mickey Logue's and Jack Simms' wonderful book *Auburn: A Pictorial History of the Loveliest Village* (now in its up to the present third edition—highly recommended). When I mentioned that book to Mr. Wright, he knew all about it, having been a valuable consultant to the authors. From his youth Mr. Wright had been what he called a "hobby" photographer, and had some vintage photographs from his school years in Auburn, the teens, some that he took, some that he is in, that are visual treasures. A shot of Vice President Thomas R. Marshall ("what this country needs is a really good five-cent cigar") on a visit to Auburn in 1915. Another from 1915 of the first class, of which he was a part, to graduate from the then new Lee County High School (Northside, and closed, in my childhood, site of the City Pool, then the Youth Center in my teens, now a memory). I must say, though the Alfonso I knew was in his eighties, I immediately recognized him. There are also a couple of photos, one looking over the top of young Toomer's Drug Store, another from the water tower in the lot just behind it, both from 1918, facing west. And a wonderful shot of the 1911 Boy Scouts on a hike at Chewacla, with a twelve-year-old Alfonso, whose services were required to identify the boys—which he did as far as his magnifying glass would allow.

* * *

When I travel from my home in LaGrange, Georgia, the forty-something miles to Auburn, where I still have friends, I drive down Highway 29 just past Long Cane Baptist Church, then turn down Gabbetville Road, cross the tracks, and catch the interstate at the KIA plant. I always do, but particularly on my last trip, as I was heading to the AU Archives to learn more about Mr. Wright, I thought of him. His mother, Susan Hudson, was from that area, and married George Wright in that church (well-preserved, overlooking the highway, with this sign out front on the day of my trip: "Praying for Youth Minister. Are You It") on a zero-degree day in the late 1890s. The wagon ruts were frozen solid, and the riding rough, as they rode to the train station right there where I so often pass, at Gabbetville, and took the afternoon train to Auburn for I guess what passed as their honeymoon. This took place in grandfather Wright's house, where North Gay Street hits Drake Avenue then gee-haws ahead—still mostly there. Grandfather Wright had moved into town by then, having lived for some prior years near his mill at Chewacla. The young couple shortly settled into their new home at 259 Opelika Road, long since a prey to the ravages of progress, where Alfonso was born on December 1, 1899. The lad grew up in those environs which at that time were the northeastern outskirts of Auburn, five blocks from the center of town, seven long miles from Opelika. W. W. Wright died in September, 1905, and Alfonso's father a year later on the boy's first day of grade school, September, 1906. The school, next to the site of the original Auburn Female Institute, was located on Tichenor Avenue where the building that was the post office during my era in Auburn, then City Hall, now sits.

* * *

Alfonso started at API in Electrical Engineering in 1916, and didn't miss much. He toted his box camera around, documenting his world, he was an artist for the yearbook, "after the Great War," he was a projectionist and reel-rewinder (25¢ a film) for the movies shown in Samford Park in front of Langdon Hall (black folks could sit behind the sheet-like screen and watch the films backwards), he attended concerts, plays, sporting events. He remembered showing *Birth of a Nation*, and in his archive materials one finds a handwritten, carefully recorded list of all the movies shown between November 24, 1915 (*The Fatal Card*) and June 2, 1917 ("Ballads of Bolgne"—presumably *Ballads and Bologna*). He was a particular fan of the Coburn Players from New York, who made annual stops in Auburn on their tours. He collected programs of their productions, mostly Shakespeare, staged "open air" in front of Samford Hall. Among his materials one also finds a newspaper clipping about Charles Coburn's death in 1961. He enjoyed a close bond with his fellow engineering students, with whom he participated in reunions until at least 1980. You can see the group photographs through the years.

I remember one afternoon standing with Mr. Wright on the walk in front of my shop, looking south, over the Alabama Power substation west of Spencer Lumber Company. He couldn't see much, but his mind's eye saw the Auburn of seventy years ago: the ice house, the railroad tracks, and just east, on Warrior

Court, the White-Harris house (sometimes referred to as the "Seven-Name House"). Three blocks away, in town (the world of Wright Brothers Book Store, and the Thomas and Jones Hotels), he imagined the water tower, in the lot between College and Gay, from which he took the photograph in 1918. He told me that every year it fell to some freshman to climb the water tower and paint the year of the senior class on the tank. And in 1916, "guess who got the job?" He made the climb with brush and bucket, none too comfortably, and once on the catwalk saw a way to save some time: he turned the "5" of last year's "1915" into a "6." Or maybe when he was a senior, he climbed up there and painted away the lower left part of the "8" to make a "9." Seems like I remember hearing both versions, and I'm not sure which is true.

Mr. Wright graduated in 1919 and moved to Pittsburgh, where he worked for Westinghouse. Then he went to Cincinnati, then Indianapolis, then West Palm Beach, Florida, in 1923 where he entered business with his classmate Lewis Vaughan. In 1928 he returned to Indianapolis as an independent electrical sales engineer, and ultimately spent thirty-five years with GE, as you may have heard. He remained in Indianapolis until the death of his second wife, Arlene, in 1979, after which he moved back to Auburn where he owned property and lived until his death in 1992.

* * *

Among the archive materials I found a typed letter written by Mr. Wright on the occasion of his donating his reminiscences and memorabilia to Auburn University in the fall of 1974. He was still living in Indianapolis then, and the letter is addressed to Dr. Floyd H. Vallery in the President's office. Its heading is vintage Mr. Wright: "11:30 PM October 22 1974."

He begins by pointing out that the letter is being written on a Royal #5, purchased second-hand in his sophomore year—in other words, a typewriter he had bought used and was still using fifty-seven years later. He observes with clear satisfaction that his class had just celebrated its fifty-five-year reunion, then goes on, in the clear and literate phrasing of pretty much all pre-electronic people, though especially exact in his case, to provide some general reflections. I remembered well that he was always astonished and exasperated at the inefficiency and ineptitude of those steering the nation's ship. He couldn't understand the lack of common sense and failure of politicians to apply simple and well-known business principles to the economy. I could hear his voice in this passage:

To give you a sample of the business acumen of classmate Vaughn [his one-time business partner], he & wife visited us in Indianapolis eight weeks ago. I asked what he did with his WW-I insurance. He had paid up the $10,000 policy. Its loan value was $7,500 so he borrowed that amount at the 5% interest charge as stated in the policy. With that $7,500 he had purchased a tax-free municipal bond which pays 7½%. The annual dividend on the insurance now is about $340, tax-free. The annual interest cost of the loan is $375 and that is deductible on Federal Income Tax. If Pres. Ford is seriously concerned over inflation, why does he not call in businessmen like that to make workable suggestions?

He wrote about his grandfather, W. W. Wright, who died in the house at the gee-haw of North Gay Street in 1905 when Alfonso was six, and who lived a ghostly life in his mind. "He sat in a wheelchair before the open fireplace, smoking cigars which his manservant lighted from the fire using a taper made of a twisted strip of newspaper to save matches." To the right of the mantel there was a closet that was off-limits to everyone except the old man. He kept his sack of gold coins in there, his drinking whiskey ("as if there were some other kind"), and his trunk containing all his records. Those contents were finally brought to light some years after his death, and meticulously described by Alfonso's cousin John Peavy Wright in his 1969 book *Glimpses Into the Past from My Grandfather's Trunk*. Mr. Wright points out that the trunk contained "every paper, receipt, document, letter, etc. that came into his possession." He might well have been speaking of himself. He adds: "The essential value of those materials arises from the extent to which they present a history of the community rather than from any personal information that might be garnered regarding the Wright family." A Rememberer, not a hoarder. And he's right about the thoroughness of the trove: Peavy Wright's book contains an excruciating account of the paper trail of the ownership of Wright's Mill, for example, descending into the depths of the nineteenth century, and a daunting catalog of various receipts from the same period, illuminating, indeed, as Mr. Wright said, the costs of daily life in that era.

Mr. Wright told the story of his uncle, John Turner Hudson, his mother's younger brother, who was working, apparently not too happily, in a machine shop in Bessemer when he got the telegram in 1906 that his brother-in-law had died. He left the work he was engaged in on his lathe, walked out, took the fastest trains to Auburn, and never returned. He came to help his sister and her young son. He stayed with them until he got married some years later. He took over Mr. Wright's dry goods store, next to Wright Brothers Bookstore, and proved a capable businessman. Alfonso attributed what business sense he had, and he had plenty, to his uncle. "I started working in his store as soon as I could ride a bicycle." He made deliveries, and remembered riding up to the train depot to get shipments off the train.

* * *

Alfonso was an only child, who married twice, and didn't have children—which simplified matters of inheritance for him, which were significant. W. W. and Mrs. Wright had thirteen children, so there were cousins aplenty, including the aforementioned John Peavy Wright (who was clubfooted and wore braces as a child; if the mule was plowing, he would *walk* the five miles to school and back—he eventually got a PhD from Harvard), and George Herbert "Monk" Wright (who served three stints, a total of nineteen years, as Auburn's mayor, and who was my landlord in the early '80s). Three of the daughters never married; W. W. Wright provided in his will a life interest in the Drake Avenue house for any unmarried children. The last one died in that house in 1951, forty-six years after her father's death. The property was probated and sold, and later, in 1953, on the day Mr. Wright, living in Indianapolis, got his check for his share, he happened to see an item in the *Indianapolis Sunday Star* concerning a tornado that had hit Auburn. It turned out the storm, the infamous tornado of '53, took off the upper story of the house and snapped off all the cedar trees about fifteen feet from the ground. A few days later, "my check plus more" went for sewer assessment, so like most acts of God, this one took its toll. The house has had a number of renters and incarnations through the years, including a daycare center, and is still there, one-story, cedar trees recovered.

* * *

I sold Village Printers in 1986 and moved to LaGrange in 1989. By then, Mr. Wright was totally blind and had moved into a nursing home. He stayed lucid as long as I knew him, but his life circumstances had forced him to cultivate his inner curmudgeon—and who could blame him? I would visit him in the nursing home, bringing whiskey, and we'd share a snort as he'd rail about the thieving idiots around him. All he could say was, thank God he had the means to afford a private room. Roommate? One of these loons around here? No thank you. When I was about to move to LaGrange to teach at the College, he told me I should contact his cousin Charles Hudson, a prominent LaGrange businessman, let him know who I was, mention himself, and so forth. I wasn't too comfortable about it, but I did it. It was only later that I came to understand who Charles Hudson was: a grandee of the first order, Callaway in-law, long time Chairman of the Board of Trustees of LaGrange College, a former interim president, and the College's all-around premier supporter. No wonder the people in the office were looking at me funny—such a brazen act of kissassery they must have marveled over after I left.

Mr. Wright, a sort of Willy Loman with resources, would have brushed it off. It's all about who you know, making connections, being liked.

I got busy again and the visits grew rarer, until the day in 1992 when I got a letter from Clark Hudson with Mr. Wright's obituary.

He was ninety-two and a half, a Rememberer, who contained a universe.

George Alfonso Wright, circa 1920s

Photograph courtesy of
Auburn University Library
Special Collections and Archives
Department

The Roses: Charles and Natalyn, circa 2004

Remembering Charlie

"The days that are no more—"
August, 2015

On paper he was Dr. Charles Rose—to everybody he knew, Charlie. He taught in the English department at Auburn from 1960 to 1994, and one of my regrets is that I never had him as a teacher. But I was compensated by having him as a friend for almost thirty years. We lost him in 2011.

My cousin Billy lucked into him for European Fiction during undergraduate days in the seventies, and offers this:

> Ah, Dr. Rose. He would sit on the corner of his desk, and smoke these cigarettes that were about a foot long. He would take these thirty-second draws, then just sit, exhaling smoke for about five minutes (it seemed). Sometimes it would take him a long, long time to answer questions. Students would start looking around, wondering if he had a stroke or something. Eventually he would answer, and it would be intelligent and thoughtful. When he returned a paper to you, it would have these little comments on it that were completely illegible. I had no idea what they said. They were like something out of *Lord of the Rings*.

Sometimes he would move over to a window and stand discoursing in his peculiar way on Kafka, Joyce, Mann, Tolstoy—an erratic monologue that would bob along on the surface, then unexpectedly dive into the depths and come up with some Coleridge-like insight, then return to the surface, or, often, to one of those protracted silences, though as with most things about Charlie not uncomfortable, just odd. By all reports this idiosyncratic performance was always interesting, and at its best, mesmerizing. Students responded to his good will; there was a lot about Charlie that was unfathomable, but nothing arrogant or threatening or cynical—nothing at all.

His son Kenneth, who once slipped into the back of one of his classes, reflects:

> He had a command of the classroom. They were discussing a poem, and I realized the gift he was giving his students. Total dedication—the energy he put into the air calling on the historical context in which the poem was written, the events in the poet's life that contributed to his work, the meanings of the complex phrases. He put something real into

that class. You left knowing that he cared, that he was a very gifted teacher, and that he had created an experience out of thin air. What you paid for. His energy made me want to tap into the wisdom, excitement, and pleasure that my father genuinely felt.

His creative writing classes enjoyed the same vibe. An accomplished short story writer himself, Charlie had spent a lifetime thinking about style, character development, dialogue. He understood the crucial distinction between what is expressed and understood. I know several people who took these classes, and they told me about the class meetings spent examining good writing, hearing Charlie read illustrations of his points, and excerpts of student writing, anonymously. But most vividly they remembered the private conferences, conducted at Jack's, Auburn's first chain hamburger joint, on the corner of College and Thach, site of The Greenhouse in my youth—that quaint thing, a boarding house—onto whose porch I had thrown the first paper of my route, a site too prime to long escape the juggernaut of improvement. Charlie ruled a booth there, drinking the first half of a million cups of coffee, framed by his characteristic disarray. Later, when Jack's fell, he migrated over to Burger King, where he met students, graded papers, did his own writing. But in the golden age, at Jack's, students would arrive at their appointed times, get a piece or two of excellent advice—"precision criticism" my friend Rheta Grimsley Johnson says—and leave with hope—in a few cases, such as Rheta's, justified.

* * *

Charlie grew up and attended high school in Kokomo, Indiana. He graduated in 1948 with highest honors. He was a gifted kid—a natural writer who was inspired to learn piano by his jazz-loving father—and who drew well enough he might have been a cartoonist. In a little autobiographical sketch, "A Rosy Life," that survives from his senior year, he notes:

> My teachers have been disillusioned as to my habits of study. To me, studying is often just an excuse to cover my paper with drawings. Two years of art have increased this mania, for after spending one period a day drawing what I am told, I find myself drawing everything else under the sun during the other six periods.

All his life Charlie's family and friends were regaled with his whimsical sketches. And we all marveled at his soldiers—his favorite era the

Napoleonic—drawn and colored with an exactness down to the buttons, pasted onto cardboard and cut out with little stands, filling an entire room like the Chinese Terracotta Army. I have a few, and a Santa Claus he once made for my kids, but the rest were lost in a fire.

After high school he headed to Vanderbilt, where his father had attended, and graduated in 1952. He went on to get an MA, then in 1954 hitchhiked with his brother Dick to New Orleans where they sold Bible supplements for two dollars down and a dollar a week, earning enough to survive like, and with, the cockroaches. With 1-A draft status he and Dick enlisted in the U.S. Army Security Agency and were assigned to language school. Charlie drew Russian and, after his training, was stationed in Washington DC. At the end of his stint in 1957, he headed for the University of Florida for doctoral work. In Gainesville he knew Harry Crews, and became something of an acolyte to Andrew Lytle. He also married his first wife Barbara in 1958, and brought her with him to his first and only teaching job at Auburn in 1960. That marriage produced Chuck and Mary, whom I barely knew.

* * *

When he arrived in Auburn, Charlie was thirty years old, and I was eight. It was only years later, when I got to know him that I began to see through his eyes the alter-Auburn that was outside my ken as I grew up.

My parents were small-town southern conservatives, even if using those words ourselves would have been like a fish talking about water—regulars at the Methodist Church in the era of Joel McDavid and Powers McCleod, and largely oblivious to the Auburn demimonde—its few watering holes and gathering places. I do remember Daddy had a co-worker named Al Hill, a name which for some reason I misconstrued throughout my childhood as Owl Hill, who had a scandalous wife, and they went to some shadowy club somewhere and *drank*—but otherwise we would ride past the Casino, or the Elks Club, or the Holiday Inn out at The Bottle, with its *lounge*, and not even see them. It's not so much that they were infamous—they were more like something barely glimpsed from an alternate dimension—about as far from the orbit of our lives as something in the same geographical space can be.

If only I could have looked inside! There I would have found the young, mustachioed Charlie—dashing, fun-loving, a ladies' man, who may not have looked like Fred Astaire but was a wonderful dancer—who entertained that hard-drinking circle of friends at the piano.

But mostly, I learned later, that carousing life, in limited Auburn, went on at parties. After a devastating divorce, he met his second wife Sandra, or rather, she met him, the morning after one of those bacchanals when she was waiting as he brought out the trash. That marriage gave us my good friends Kenneth and Josephine, both flourishing today with copious progeny, holding the memory of their father dear. Charlie was just one of the brilliant, eccentric academic personalities of that era before academia had been emasculated by technocratic micro-control—many legendary, the kind of teachers you never forgot—who bonded together in their off-time and pursued the time-honored diversions of conversation, hanky-panky, and strong waters. My friend Hines Hall, who came into the Auburn History department in 1967 as a young instructor still working on his Vanderbilt dissertation, back when English and History were still housed in Samford Hall, has filled in for me some of the details of that colorful era and its personalities—Charlie, Madison Jones, Oxford Stroud, Bob Rea, Tom Belser, and many others—when I was knocking around barefoot stealing plums, or cruising around Auburn with Mama in the Buick, and Charlie and his cohorts were living hard in an adjacent universe. Hines, who moved in that circle, had first met Charlie while still at Vanderbilt, when Charlie had come up with the fencing club for a match. By all accounts Charlie was no mean fencer. Like tennis—when I found out he played, and we decided to have a go at it, I figured he'd be easy to deal with. Wrong. Very wrong. He may not have looked like Rod Laver, but you hit the ball to Charlie, he hit it back.

The dimensions began to coalesce into a more complex whole later when Charlie and I became good friends.

In the early eighties, when I had come back to Auburn after several wandering years, and started a printing business, Charlie and his third wife Natalyn, a talented painter of some renown and still one of my close friends, lived in the other half of an old house on North Gay Street they shared with some other friends of mine. Natalyn came to work for me as a typesetter, and we all got acquainted. I discovered the Charlie of report—the thought-gathering, the bursts of brilliance, the humor, the dithery eccentricity, the gentle magnanimity.

We had a lot of friends in the Art department, and during the eighties and into the nineties we gathered at Charlie and Natalyn's house on West Bowden Drive, and on most Friday afternoons at the Thach Avenue *salon* of Agnes Taugner. Those were incredibly rich days, surely a twenty-year later version of the get-togethers of Charlie's early Auburn years. Artists, writers, musicians—a world where creativity was common, an endless spigot of personalities, and laughter. A lot of laughter. As I've said elsewhere, if you want to get to the soul, follow the laughter. It was the kind of time which, as always, you think couldn't possibly ever end, and which, as always, proves to be ephemeral.

Still in my memorial heart, there's something about an old southern house, with a big porch, pecan trees outside, friends, libations, laughter, and music within.

Later, Charlie and Natalyn moved to Cary Drive. By then I had relocated to LaGrange, was married with young children, and many of the other personalities had moved on. But those times, though less-peopled, were no less rich.

We would come into that house, almost tripping over the art everywhere—Natalyn's paintings, various work of her friends—Natalyn with a martini would just be chopping up celery or something for the dinner we would eventually eat—and Charlie would greet us in a way you knew he was genuinely glad to see you, as you were him. The house would be in the state of amiable but hopeless dishevelment that was part of their being—plants everywhere, a cat or two, piles, stacks, heaves of everything, on the piano, on tables, shelves, the floor, a million books, most filled with Charlie's spidery runes. We would start talking and wouldn't stop until we carried the sleeping kids out to the car at midnight and headed home. What did we talk about? God, I don't know—everything. Books, music, people. An article one of us had just read. Or maybe it was that most wonderful situation where we'd all just read the same thing and had strong opinions—the chances excellent—no, certain—that Charlie and Natalyn would disagree. "Oh, Charlie!" Natalyn would exasperatedly exclaim, silencing, but never changing, him. We just talked—I don't think I could ever get tired of talking with Charlie.

Though to be honest, often I listened—because Charlie knew more about literature than I did. He was one of the best-read people I've ever met. He had read everything. And *remembered* it. A mutually favorite author was Joyce (whom we both idolized and Natalyn thought over-rated)—or we could talk about southern writers, or Tom Wolfe, or James Wood's criticism; or Charlie could tell you things about Thomas Mann, Raymond Chandler (whom he loved), or Gaddis, or Pynchon. He'd read it all.

I'd bring beer. He'd always have some bourbon, some good scotch. And, of course, those martinis.

* * *

One night, not long before I moved to LaGrange, I brought my drums and a bass-playing friend over to his house on Bowden Drive, and we set up around his piano and had some fun. Shortly after, as chance would have it, a long ago student of his, Bill Green, then a professor himself, a poet, and the closest thing to a beatnik I've ever known, got in touch with him, and before long we were trekking over to Bill's house in Phenix City on Friday nights to play. Not just an old, but in this case antebellum, house with an historical plaque, just off Summerville Road, which Bill later painted lilac. By then, I had gotten to know another of the great friends of my life, Roger Hagerty, whose brother Bob, an artist, had been a regular at those affairs at Agnes's house—in fact, her live-in. Roger played sax and he started playing with us, and then Bill brought over the choir director from his church, Bonnie Adams, to sing. We became The Little Big Band, and before long Roger and Bonnie got together, and eventually married.

I can't remember exactly how long it lasted—three or four years, I guess, but it was another of those charmed islands of time. Bill's wife Katy, who taught English at Auburn, was very accommodating and supportive. She and Bill had two sons, Aaron and Nathan, both musicians, and I can remember a few Friday evenings when we would be downstairs, and their respective bands would be in two rooms upstairs, all practicing. That lilac house shook the historic district. We played the songs Charlie knew, old standards—Porter, Gershwin, Mercer, Carmichael, Rodgers and Hart, and the like. We turned Charlie loose on "Won't You Come Home, Bill Bailey," his featured vocal, which he belted out with great piano-pounding gusto. As I said, Charlie wasn't arrogant—it's not that he disparaged or looked down on other genres of music—they just didn't do it for him. He was all about Tin Pan Alley, show tunes, jazz. The music was great, and the breaks around the kitchen table almost as much fun.

We were never better than fair, but we had our moments. That old house served us well—we were having a ball, and then, the inevitable: Bill decided we were ready to go public. I resisted, but to no avail. Next thing you know, he had booked us at the Phenix City Moose Club. We dressed up and played, but to be honest, the only impression I retain of that gig is a scowling drill sergeant-like cook who made it clear she didn't like us one bit.

That sort of set the tone for our live performance career. Bill kept finding us places to play, and he was one of these booking agents who would promise anything. Latin American band? Of course! That got us into a Mexican restaurant where we added "Acércate Más" and "La Bamba" to the set list, and even attempted to get the poor burrito-eating diners into a conga line, weaving among the tables. At one point we played at the Columbus Jazz Society at the Hilton where we did about as well as we ever did, then were followed by the pick-up band, a group of kick-ass jazz players.

* * *

After my first graduation from Auburn I had drifted around for a couple of years, then exhausted from living hand to mouth, and still with many friends in Auburn, I came back to the refuge of graduate school in the mid/late seventies. Rheta has told me about the condescension she endured at Auburn as a journalism major from the English crowd. My God. I caught scents of various species of condescension myself during my graduate days. I detected among some of the other graduate students, not my friends, an undercurrent of ridicule toward Charlie, in his prime then, but apparently an out-of-touch relic to them, in this period when English departments everywhere were busy trying to talk themselves out of their own subject matter. I didn't know Charlie then, but date our bond from that period. If *they* didn't like him, he must be okay.

Charlie was drawn to what is *interesting* about literature and writers, with his own categories, and he had plenty to keep him busy for a lifetime. Charlie's fascination with psychology, history, technique, served him well and made him the kind of person with whom you could sit up half the night talking. Writing was a living art form for him. If the author is dead, then so is fiction writing itself—at least as a broad-based viable cultural vehicle. When you get to the point where you say do it like this, never like that; always say this, never say that—when you're more aware of the doing than what is done—you're dealing with a dead art form. Having something to say—storytelling—these are and always will be alive and well—but the vessel evolves. Obviously that function is performed primarily by television today. Tomorrow it will be cerebrocams. We've picked writing to death.

Charlie wouldn't necessarily have agreed with me about all this, nor about the post-mortem role provided by the fiction seminar. He wasn't really a maverick; he worked mainly within the system. He himself had attended Bread Loaf and Sewanee, a Tennessee Williams Scholar at the latter in 1999, and he got a lot out of those experiences. He was also awarded an Alabama State Council on the Arts Fellowship for literary arts/fiction in 2004. It's not as though his accomplishments as a writer went unrecognized. And he didn't share with me my longing for a writing completely unaware of itself—an achievement of—that is, a return to—that prelapsarian state where I wrote for fun and to entertain myself and my friends, with no sense of duty or obligation, and the thought of Being a Writer had never entered my head. I remember one night at my house in LaGrange when Charlie had had more than a few and was standing in my back yard declaiming with wounded, defiant zeal, more or less to the sky, on the importance of just that: *Being a Writer.*

As a short story writer, Charlie was a master of the quiet epiphany—influenced by many writers, but if you wanted to name a principal influence, you might say Raymond Carver. Charlie published his short stories all over, twenty-eight in all. He got into Lytle's *Sewanee Review*, and into one of their greatest hits collections. The best were collected in *A Ford in the River*, published posthumously. They are the kind of stories you must read carefully—he had a strong inclination toward understatement, and the power always lay under the surface. You have to tune in to his frequency; if your mind wanders, you miss something. What he has to say is never emphasized—it sits quietly and looks like everything else.

He had this literary devotion in common with Andrew Lytle, though he didn't exactly share the Agrarian ethic. Charlie was a town man, urbane, and unlike Lytle, who really was a farmer, or at least a serious gardener, he didn't have much to do with dirt. The Agrarians were focused on what was lost as the overcrowded twentieth century industrial world threatened the human spirit, the very validity of the idea of the "human spirit" itself. They were prescient about the despoliation of the natural environment collateral to this process. Like Gandhi they now seem a little naïve in their faith in the village life. The ideas of revolutionaries always come with the implicit belief that human beings will change their nature to accommodate them. I can't say I see a shred of evidence for that.

The coming digital world was in a lot of ways contrary to Charlie's essence. He retired from teaching in 1994, a year before the death of Lytle, before computers had completely taken over, before bureaucratic overkill had stifled the creativity of teaching, and though he was comfortable enough at a keyboard, one can't help seeing in Charlie a particularly clear illustration of the gain/loss trade-off that provoked the Agrarians.

A couple of hypothetical scenarios:

Charlie teaching an on-line course. It's fair to say that everything good about him would be lost. The whole point about Charlie was his Charlieness, and he was at his best face to face with other human beings. He was odd, but he was social. As I've tried to show, it was a joy to be around him. To trade that for an on-line transfer of information is an idea so barbaric one can hardly consider it. I'm not sure the rich silences would play well in an on-line environment either. What he purveyed wasn't really *information* anyway—it was spiritual value. Which is another way of saying he dealt with what was *interesting*.

Can't eat that, they'll say.

I say, then life is not worth living. And we'll no longer have to worry about the automatons we're so afraid are going to take our jobs and make human existence superfluous—we will have already turned into them ourselves.

Second scenario—what if during those countless rich conversations with Charlie he had been all the while checking tweets, Facebook, tennis scores, snapchats, and googling arcana? I probably wouldn't even remember him, because he wouldn't really have been with me. Just as I know my most recent students won't remember me, because I was only one of about a dozen channels they had going in my classes, and tuned in to me only in pulses, when I pavloved them with some word like "test" or said something funny. Ha ha—change channel.

What we seem to be losing is personality.

Personality has become a commodity, an option, and we have so many curtains to hide ourselves behind now. Dealing with personality, projecting our own, requires energy—but our energy today is spread thin.

When you were with Charlie, he was with you completely, and he listened to you. He was never one of those people who stop listening and start nodding their heads about halfway through what you're saying because they've already identified a category to put your ideas in, and are impatient to blurt out their own. Charlie lived less in a pre-fab intellectual world than most people—he took the world as it came. That is why those graduate students sneered, and why he retired as an associate professor (emeritus)—he hadn't bought the code. And he didn't play by the pre-fab rules, and when you don't, the bureaucrats withhold their pellets, and give your inferiors, who mistake learning that code for intelligence, a green light to enjoy some cheap condescension.

What I loved most about Charlie was his dominant defining trait: his humor. Charlie was very funny. Sometimes unintentionally. One night we were driving home from a party—my then-wife and Natalyn in the back seat, Charlie in the passenger seat, and Natalyn started rhapsodizing about how she had been attracted to Charlie in large measure because he was the smartest man she knew, he all the while engaged in trying to close my uncloseable glove compartment door. *Brilliant!*—*plop*. *Intelligent!*—*plop*. *Creative!*—*plop*. Or his long, wandering voicemail messages, when he would run out of tape still nowhere near his point. Or the time his dog kept digging up the cat he had just buried, so he took it to the AU vet clinic in the middle of the night for them to dispose of, but finding no one, put the lamented feline in the night depository (according to some sources—Natalyn claims it never happened). True, I saw him mostly on weekends, in leisure time—but when I was with him it seemed he was always either laughing or about to. He never got his drawers in a knot. I don't think I ever saw him in a hurry.

* * *

After retiring, Charlie worked on his own projects—his stories, screenplays with his brother Dick, and I don't know what all. He read, he played the piano, and in 1997 he became a Hospice volunteer. In 1998 he was Hospice Volunteer of the Year. That experience, visiting the dying, resulted in a book, *In the Midst of Life*, where he told the stories but changed the names. Maybe in a way that experience helped steel him for the difficulties that lay ahead for him personally.

In 2004 he developed cancer of the bladder, which made life complicated, but he took it in stride. Then in 2008 he had a stroke, and though I wasn't involved in the early painful process of his rehabilitation, I do remember his later, extraordinary efforts to regain his ability to read. The progress he made was almost superhuman. He was in Oak Park, an assisted living facility, then, and the first thing to come back was his piano playing. The other residents were glad—as he had me, he had given them something to do.

Then he moved to a nursing home where, at least when I visited him, he retained his good spirits, and then in 2011 he left us.

That's when the harmless saying "feel like I've lost my best friend" became real for me—particularly as it happened four months after I was devastated by the sudden loss of Roger, and only a month before the loss of my mother. Another saying—"they come in threes"—became real. I am still blessed with good friends—thank God!—but I lost two of the best pals I ever had, and the most influential person in my life, in one blow. What does that feel like? Well—nothing. You just don't have as many places to go and fewer reasons to talk out loud. One of the most touching passages in all of literature is the "lament of the last survivor" in *Beowulf*—where the survivor describes what it feels like when your place, your time, your people are all gone. It's the potential fate of us all. And sublimely poetic. Our pain, like gold hammered into enameling, lives a second life as poetry.

Josephine and Kenneth consulted me and some other friends and family members about a quotation for Charlie's grave marker. We settled on "And gather me into the artifice of eternity"—perfect, I think—Yeats's weariness with the cycle of mortality, and his faith in the eternity of the realized soul. Charlie is buried in Town Creek cemetery, exactly where I used to play—who knows?—maybe my young feet passed over the very spot—a block from my childhood home, a lifetime from his in Kokomo.

* * *

"There is no greater sorrow than remembering in misery the happy time."

Charlie loved Dante. Who knows how many times he taught him in thirty-four years? I can still hear his voice, but as I trudge ahead in this post-best friend world, only in echoes.

I wouldn't know where to look to find somebody like him now.

Little Big Band, 1991
Front row (l-r): Charlie, Bonnie Adams, Roger Hagerty, Pedro Rodriguez
Back row: Bill Green, me

Mrs. Umbach

Photograph courtesy of Susan Haines

Photograph courtesy of Susan Haines

Mrs. Metzger's Class
(This was a class a little before my time.)

Mrs. Webster's Class
(Me, front and center)

Mrs. Meagher's Kindergarten Class
(Me, back row, far left)

My First Seven Teachers
February, 2016

Seven women from the past—no doubt all gone from the earth now—still guard the gates of my childhood, and are a part of me: my kindergarten and elementary school teachers. I have long felt that, excepting my family, that group of matrons was the strongest formative influence of my life. It's not so much that I think of them often, as that they are indelibly ingrained in the primordial scenes of my life, and to think at all is to sense their presence. As a society we rarely recognize the enormity of our primary teachers' impact, and still don't hold them in the proper estimation—in the land of Donald Trump, there's nothing shocking in that. My purpose here is not political, to argue that they should receive something back from society more proportionate to what they put in—to me that's obvious—but poetic: an attempt to pry something out of the heart with words.

Mrs. Meagher, Mrs. Umbach, Mrs. Lane, Mrs. Metzger, Mrs. Hagler, Mrs. Webster, Mrs. Green: my own memorial Mt. Rushmore. All about the age then of my own grandmothers, and with that same grandmotherly quality. And all women, needless to say. The men were principals, superintendents, and other Important things. Bureaucrats. They never entered classrooms but made the rules; the women lived in the classrooms and some may have actually followed them. I never questioned that arrangement at the time—I was a kid and not into questioning. But I've devoted some thought to it since. I think the fact that women were entrusted, or rather, left with, the responsibility of instilling the dominant cultural vision into our young proves that we are a more matriarchal society than we recognize. We intuitively gave this vital underpaid job to the best people to do it, and made men overpaid bureaucrats to get them out of the way. The best way to nullify something is to make it Important.

But, as I said, let's not go there. I am only after the phantoms.

* * *

It's not really surprising, I guess, given the way life condenses itself away, how few specific memories I retain of the seven ladies: a handful of static scenes, some short mental videos, a smattering of smells, sounds. But in a way that's the point: just as Yeats became his admirers, they have become their influence. The actual physical life of something is such a fractional part of its existence—its resonance in everything it affected is far greater. But I do remember some bits and pieces, and set out on a quest to discover some more. A not particularly fruitful quest, on the surface, but one that took some interesting turns.

* * *

The first roadblock I hit was the discovery that there are no official records or pictures of that era anywhere—or at least anywhere I thought to look. So I was left with ransacking my memory, asking childhood classmates for input, sending out electronic pleas, and looking through a shoebox fourteen times for the picture of Mrs. Umbach I know is—or was—in there, but now seems to have disappeared. Everybody I talked to gave me a morsel or two, or triggered something long forgotten within me. I was either lucky, or am a good mythmaker, because I remember all the ladies, with the exception of the formidable Mrs. Metzger and the Nazgul-like substitute teacher Miss Smith, as benign and affectionate—but in talking to old classmates I was reminded that not everyone shares the mental process by which I personally have rendered that era into the idyllic register. The fact is, whoever the lady might have been, and to whatever extent your own chemistry might have been compatible with hers, you were stuck with her for nine months with no real recourse in a world that offered no escape routes for those out of harmony with it. I didn't say the influence was always good—just that it was strong.

Jimmy Lyle, for example—away from school a fun and funny kid, my friend—but my childhood's poster child for maladjustment. He didn't care for authority, particularly not in the form of these hags with so much power over him, and he wasn't afraid to show it. They'd call it some name now. Or my friend Art Fourier, who attended Cary Woods, and remembers nausea on Sunday afternoons, dreading the return of Monday and its waiting Gorgon. One teacher who, if she caught you chewing gum, made you stick it on your nose, one who wielded a bolo paddle—with the staple still in it!—the scarlet talons of another, gouging into young shoulders, and many who wielded rulers. Or my friend Lauren Lancaster who remembers her third grade teacher Mrs. Robertson as "terrible and mean" and retains above all a memory of being dragged by the ear across the room in her terrifying grip. Lauren also recalls her dealing with a troublesome boy by tying him to his desk with a jump rope while the rest of the class went out to play. It wasn't all roses for me either; let's just say, sitting in little desks with pencils the size of tree trunks learning arithmetic and reading does not come naturally to children—but for me the tide of time has eroded away most of the bad.

I attended Mrs. Meagher's kindergarten, and Samford Avenue for grades one through four, and Wrights Mill Road for grades five and six. The other schools in town were Cary Woods, Dean Road, and for a time, Northside. I didn't get to know Art, or many other kids from those other schools, except in Sunday school or Boy Scouts or something, until seventh grade when we all converged on Samford Avenue. The crosstown teachers had a half-real, alien quality—the gigglingly-named Mrs. Bottoms at the "other" kindergarten; Mrs. Harris, my neighbor on Brookside, a pleasant lady off-duty but reputed to deserve that most terrifying of adjectives when on: *strict*; or the Dean Road name that I heard much of in school days and that not surprisingly surfaced in many recollections: Mrs. Vowell. Thanks to those recollections I now have a mental picture of a well-dressed vibrant and loveable middle-aged teacher in heels—my friend Donna Bohanan has evoked the name of June Cleaver and thus banished any other possibility—going around to a variety of stations and feeding the feral cats of Auburn. She seems also to have had an occasional dog in her classroom, one that perhaps followed one of her scholars to school, requiring periodic hiding from the authorities. Alas that I never had her.

* * *

After meeting with much frustration in my attempts to find out some specific information about my own seven ladies, I resigned myself to the impressionistic, aided by my investigations. And then—a bolt of good fortune. A chance remark by a friend led to an introduction to a most remarkable lady—Mrs. Ruth Williamson. Ruth is ninety-four, possessed of sharp mind and memory, and thoroughly charming. A native of New York, she moved with her family to Orlando in elementary school, then landed in Montgomery with her Air Force husband Ed Williamson, a veteran of D-Day, after the war. She taught in Montgomery schools, then in 1958 moved to Auburn where Ed taught in the AU History department, and Ruth began teaching at Dean Road. She later became principal of that school, played a key role in the racial integration of the schools in the sixties, and retired in 1974. She also lived in the Bermans' old house on Woodfield, just a few houses down from the Ur-locale of my life—and cleanly fielded every name I threw at her, even if I couldn't quite do the same in return. Though she didn't work in the schools I attended, she knew most of my teachers, and generally offered a perspective that enhanced and corrected my own memories. One of her most memorable attributes is her hearty laugh, which she used in response to many of the people I mentioned. A few prompted an immediate "Oh Law!" that marked them like nothing else could. Mrs. Williamson would be the last person in the world to speak ill of anyone, but I was equally impressed with her honesty.

She was a dedicated teacher who strove to reach every child and never laid a hand on one. "If you do, you admit defeat, and I wasn't going to be defeated." But then she ran into Jimmy Seibold, brother of Eddie, Auburn's infamous murderer. "He was one of the few children I felt I didn't get to at all. He was very bright and he knew he was brighter than others. When he told the class [before Eddie's rampage] that he was going to move, they all started clapping, spontaneously. I thought that was sad, but he made it hard for me, I can tell you."

It helps to add that Mrs. Williamson, who was known to run interference for Mrs. Vowell, once kept a dog in her room too. "We gave him grades. But the children weren't allowed to pet him when they were supposed to be doing their work."

* * *

I have told the story elsewhere of my first day of kindergarten—hard in the bearhug of Mrs. Meagher and watching Mama walk away down that sloping brick drive. That moment—which indeed is all it was—was a traumatic experience, and then, like everything, it was over. She had done battle with me and won. That fact became the foundation of our relationship: she was in control, she knew, she had the truth, the answers—which meant that I didn't have to worry about all that, but could devote my energy fully to playing and learning. This is, of course, exactly the authority that children need. I know that, and have done my turn playing that role myself, but I admit I still side with the wounded child. He got what he needed to survive, yes, but in submitting to a social force lost some of his self and stepped right into the human dilemma. You get over it but you don't forget it.

All of us who attended Mrs. Meagher's kindergarten, that little kingdom sandwiched behind her house and others on East Glenn, the Church of Christ, and the back of Sonny Fields' Shell station and the Alabama Power Company office, were always aware of the sporadic presence of Red Meagher, the husband, and a sort of wacky Mr. Greenjeans handyman—a funny character to me, even if remembered in some quarters today as a gadfly and a bit of a ne'er-do-well. Red Meagher had moved from Birmingham to Auburn at a young age to live with his aunts, came through the Auburn school system, and attended API in the twenties. It was there that he got lucky—that is, met Luckie Thomas, also from the Birmingham area, and they were married in 1928. Red and Luckie opened "The Doll House" restaurant in 1939, ran it briefly, then sold it to Archie McKee. McKee, later proprietor of "Archie's," operated it for several years—my uncle remembered eating there in the forties—then eventually the little house became the iconic Sani-Freeze, or Sani-Flush to locals, dear in the memory of many who lived in Auburn during that era, but bulldozer-fodder in the end. Luckie ran the restaurant, and Red worked in construction, and when they sold the restaurant he refashioned a building behind their house into a kindergarten. Mrs. Meagher ran it from 1941 until she retired in 1977.

Like most of my teachers, Mrs. Meagher had that irresistible quality of authority grounded in love. All great teachers possess that perfect balance. It's a delicate matter—too much authority you're a tyrant; too much love, you're weak. She taught ABCs and arithmetic, turned us loose with our aprons on those tables creatively, but more importantly she embodied decency and honesty and responsibility and hard work. None of us, including Mrs. Meagher, went around thinking she was embodying those qualities; she was just following her instinct, and we absorbed it all too completely to be aware of it. She was fifty-two years old when I had her—not a big woman, sprightly, stern, kind, and funny, with some kind of wire-rimmed granny glasses and these schoolmarmish dresses. She had a bell and ran the show. I'm pretty sure she ran it at home too. I remember the construction paper, the scissors, the paste—which unlike some people I could name, I was never tempted to eat—the little green filecard boxes with our names written on them in fingernail polish—ditto our tin drink cups—graham crackers, Ritz crackers, grape juice, and apple juice. Especially apple juice. Kindergarten was the first time I ever tasted it, and to this day its flavor cohabits a neural cubicle with Mrs. Meagher. Jimmy Sprayberry remembers her always sucking on lemons, but I admit I've lost that.

The playground outside had sandboxes, monkey bars, gender-separated swings, a little wooded strip along the rear, hard by the train tracks, a block from the station. As I've said elsewhere, I'm sure that's where I developed my fascination with trains as those sleek silver and blue cars slid into the station. The coolest thing that Mrs. Meagher did, and it was a tradition with all her classes, was to take us on a train ride to Opelika where we toured an ice cream plant—Foremost maybe?—and then back. I remember being issued one of those little cups of ice cream with the flat wooden spoon. That playground is lodged in the dream center of my memory—the only photograph I know of it is our class picture in 1958 which I can stare at for hours. All of the mysteries of life coalesce there. It is mirrored twelve years later by the class photo of us as graduating high school seniors—those reunions another Mrs. Meagher tradition. The main thing I remember is that Mrs. Meagher remembered me. She remembered everybody. We had to grow up to understand how dear we had been to her—and how bittersweet her retirement must have been. She was seventy-two years old when she called it quits and must have been tired—but what was she without her kindergarten? I can't imagine, but she lived eighteen more years. Red died in 1980. The last time I saw her was in a hallway at the Wesley Terrace nursing home where my grandmother was near the end of her life, in 1992. Mrs. Meagher was coming down the hall on a walker, a key safety-pinned to her dress, her mind obviously clouded by the dementia of age. I knew her immediately, of course, and exclaimed, "Mrs. Meagher!" She stopped, looked blankly at me, then a radiant recognition came over her features—thirty-four years vanished—then she sank once more into oblivion.

Mrs. Williamson on Mrs. Meagher: "She was quite a bit older than I and had been teaching kindergarten a long time before I came. Everybody thought she was so wonderful, and the other teachers respected her. I didn't really know her that well, but I had a lot of fond feelings for her because I had heard so many nice things about her."

* * *

Of my six elementary school teachers, apart from Mrs. Metzger, probably the strongest personality was Mrs. Umbach. Indeed, I remember her more vividly than any of the others. She was the same age as Mrs. Meagher, and was fifty-three when I was in first grade. I've mentioned how I chanced upon her gravesite, beside that of her husband Swede Umbach, AU wrestling coach, and near my parents', and learned that she died in 1999. Strange—she lived to be 94, and I knew her less than a year of that. Of her long, crowded, eventful life, I had only nine months—but more than enough to leave a monument in my memory.

Mrs. Umbach was soft and plump, like a human cumulus cloud, pillowy but capable of spits of lightning—she was not above lining up the entire misbehaving class for a group bolo paddle whack. Whoever did the casting for *A Christmas Story* got the type exactly right, if ten years younger. I remember her room, the southeastern corner room of the Samford annex, later inhabited by the Fury, Mrs. Haggard. It had the alphabet on cards above the chalkboard, a flag to which we pledged allegiance daily—and I think it was during that year that I came into some dim understanding that our nation wasn't "invisible"—a trash can that looked like the nose cone of a missile in a wire frame, daily emptied by janitor Ben Dumas, who also sprinkled that red powder on the floor, especially after a vomit clean-up, before sweeping, the fragrance of which is the olfactory definition of that building—that, and the smells of the greenhouse-windowed lunch room on the opposite end of the hall—an odor so distinctive I freeze at anything even vaguely redolent of it—which is almost never. It is a vanished smell—I sought it vainly in my children's elementary school—not the same.

Ah, the black-felt menu board with insertable white letters that announced the day's fare. Fried chicken, when you prayed, usually to no avail, for a good piece, spaghetti with cheese squares on top, hamburgers, Salisbury steak, fish sticks on Fridays, corn, beans, tiny whole potatoes. Those green trays, round white milk tokens, square black meal tokens ("Auburn City Schools/Good for One Complete Meal")—often chewed—originally 25¢, causing an outrage when they went up to 40¢—then 50¢!—the steamy window where you took your tray, the midsection and arms of the woman with the industrial sprayer, faceless, like a cartoon, one whose brown pigment had leached to white—a multifarious signature smell that has become meaningful only in its loss. Lunch itself, tastes being various, often involved New York Stock Exchange-level bartering. I remember once somebody's cherry cobbler was up for auction—the trading was brisk, and at last I couldn't stand the suspense, grabbed the goop in my fist and crammed it into my mouth. Illegal, but effective.

I remember catching on quickly to phonics in first grade and easily learning to read and write. It is amazing now to reflect that, yes, one does have to *learn* to read and write at some point (Drop the "e", add "ing"!). Learning about vowels holding syllables together, consonants surrounding them and forming the basic units of speech, and its written representation, I am sure was the foundation of my later interest in linguistics and grammar, which I taught for many years. I was dimly aware that phonics later became controversial somehow—probably another example of bureaucrats who didn't actually teach it improving something that worked extremely well—I don't know. But I remember sitting in the little reading circle, anxiously awaiting my turn. Somehow one memory stands out—a page or two ahead of where we were in a story (of course I looked ahead) the mother was calling the children and her speech began with "Yoo hoo!" I knew that! And doubted anyone else would! I calculated—yes, it looked like it could well land on me! I trembled with anticipation. Then Mrs. Umbach failed to stop Jan Andrews where she *should* have, and Jan just went ahead and read "Yoo hoo!" as casually as you please. I was crushed.

Those stories! I would pay some serious money to get my hands on that reader. But I can't even find out what it was. The Internet hasn't been much help. Search first grade readers and you get mostly Dick and Jane and Spot. But I seem to remember the dog being named Tip. Turns out there's a series featuring Jack and Janet, Tip and Mitten. Could it have been that? I especially remember two or three of the stories; one featured popcorn balls, which I had never heard of and which fascinated me. I went home and peeled an orange and pretended it was a "popcorn ball." Years later, when I ran into the real thing, I admit I was a little disappointed. Reality is no match for imagination—we learn that early. Another concerned a boy who was sick and couldn't go to the parade—but it turned out the parade came right down his street where from his upstairs window he had the best seat of all! And another dealt with a woman taking a group of children fishing. Each wore a different colored hat to help her keep tabs on them. When it came time to leave, and the mother or teacher or whatever she was counted off all the colors, violet was missing. Oh dear. The mystery persisted until at last someone pointed out she herself was wearing it! Also a book, I think, about a family that had to live in a docked streetcar, which captivated me. Billy Goats Gruff, Little Black Sambo, the Troll—whatever that was—under the bridge. Many others. Mrs. Umbach—calling out our names in turn, correcting our stumbles.

My friend Mindy McCain remembers Mrs. Umbach letting children who were afraid bury their heads in her lap when we had to get shots. I'm thinking this would have been girls mostly. A touching image, but one which, I'm afraid, evokes the most horrifying experience of grade school. Shot Day.

Oh, they were terrifying, those women—battle-hardened, merciless, in stiff white dresses processing us like cattle. Clearly innovation was needed in the world of hypodermics—but it hadn't come yet when we were lambs filing by for the slaughter. You could see *your* needle waiting in the little slotted glass dish, the thick glass syringes, the smell of alcohol. To this day the words "typhoid booster" give me the same feeling as seeing a snake. Booster? Why didn't they just give you enough in the first place?

More vividly than the classroom, unsurprisingly, I remember "play period" in the first grade. We didn't call it "recess"—that was a foreign, rather pretentious word that didn't fit—sort of like somebody answering roll with "present" rather than "here," or like when the Three Stooges came on and it wasn't Curly Joe but Shemp—though I do remember the execrable substitute Miss Smith using the term "Indian recess"—because we were supposed to be as quiet as Indians in the forest. Sure. The main thing I remember about play period was how long it was—a fact which tells you something about the nerves of middle-aged women dealing with twenty grade school children, and also belies the old adage that time flies when you're having fun. They would let us go on for what seemed like hours, out there on the field behind the Samford Avenue band room, and in the creek and woods beyond, as they sat there, a group of them, on that concrete slab on the back corner of the band room. I can remember dreading the whistle, and trying to stay as far away as possible so that I could argue in court that I hadn't heard it. Like her red pencils with the red band around the gold tip, which you could not find in the dime store or anywhere, Mrs. Umbach's whistle was absolutely unique. In the box where her picture is supposed to be, I found six whistles Daddy ordered me from the Herter's catalog. Perfectly good whistles, but I could never make him understand that they weren't the same. Apparently only Mrs. Umbach had Mrs. Umbach's whistle.

She wore a distinctive hand lotion—I believe if I smelled it today I would be like Coleridge catching a hint of his damsel's symphony and song—which half the class gave her for Christmas. But not me. Mama had picked out a jarful of pecans for her gift, and wrapped it. The students took their presents to her desk where she delightedly tried to guess what they were, with an extraordinary success rate. "Lotion!" She shook my cylindrical present—it rattled like a maraca—and I swear I can still see and hear this as vividly as the day it happened—beamed at me and immediately guessed, "Pecans!" Wow.

Mrs. Umbach resides in my memory, a distinctive personality, but also larger than a mere human being—like George Washington or something. I don't remember her, or any of my teachers really, trying to indoctrinate us with their political or religious views (though Mrs. Vowell was famous for asking her students on Monday if they'd gone to church on Sunday). But if they had, we would have been defenseless, with no real social apparatus to combat it.

Especially Mrs. Umbach.

"Oh Law!" Mrs. Williamson remembers that primordial personage as a very self-assured, old-school teacher not deficient in a high opinion of herself.

Well, of course, I was six and didn't really have much to compare her to. But now that you mention it, maybe that air of authority was a bit on the imperious side. Filing by her throne to present our gifts?

* * *

I'm afraid from this point the detail of these reflections is going to fall off. My memory has relinquished much, and my detective work has been uneven.

Mrs. Lane, my second grade teacher, had almost completely faded to an elderly bespectacled white head behind a desk when I began this project. I seemed to remember her mostly sitting—a mild and gentle woman, with a rural flavor about her.

I came up with nothing in the AU Archives, until John Varner suggested I look in the City Directory. I didn't know what that was—but it turned out to be an annual volume that listed and gave a little information about all the citizens of town. I selected 1960 and, through their husbands, all of whom were connected with the university, found all my teachers—with the exception of Mrs. Webster. More on her later.

I don't know how, but I knew where all my teachers lived, and that Mrs. Lane lived in a little brick house on Wire Road, in what is now the short section between Samford and University, and can remember pointing out, whenever we drove by there, "There's Mrs. Lane's house!" Of course, today no trace of it remains. So I looked for "Lane" on Wire Road, and, happily, found only one: Hiram Lane ("formn API"). And his wife: Nola.

Nola! Nola Lane! Hiram and Nola—they could have been a painting.

Immediately her static portrait in my mind quickened into personality—she became a film clip instead of a still. I could feel again her soft voice, an excellent thing in woman, her benevolence, her humor, her gentle authority, almost hear her voice—all from a name.

She must have gotten to her feet sometimes, but that's not how I remember her. In my mind she sits behind her desk, calmly explaining something, or reading to us. I'm thinking there was a touch of dry humor about her. I would remember her as a person of total calm if not for the episode of Jimmy Lyle chasing her with a pair of scissors and scaring her half to death. I'm not sure what the upshot of that episode was, but hey, he was Jimmy Lyle. Always flirting with reform school, always back the next day. I colorfully recall, again via smell, the boy's bathroom at the south end of the hall, a medieval dungeon, the open entrance to which teachers would step just inside to quell the commotion that regularly erupted from this one place where they couldn't go. Well, except for Mrs. Metzger, who would just barge in like Special Forces coming for bin Laden. One such commotion was caused by Jimmy Lyle in there one day at his discovery of some unexplained doo-doo on the floor. As children will, when bodily functions are involved, we over-reacted, and the event resulted in a ruckus far beyond what it deserved. I remember Jimmy drooling with laughter as he explained to Mrs. Lane what he had seen: "Grease!"

Call Ben Dumas.

Mrs. Williamson hadn't known Mrs. Lane and could only verify that, yes, there had been such a person.

Unobtrusive Nola.

* * *

It's amazing how many of my teachers' names fit who they were. "Luckie" Meagher, with something of the leprechaun about her. Mrs. Haggard, the Gorgon. The quiet and rustic Mrs. Lane. But it was not until many years later, when I studied German, that I learned what "Metzger" meant.

I never saw her with a cleaver, so I don't know—but let's just say, it fit.

I'm pretty sure I never saw Mrs. Metzger laugh. I certainly didn't try any of my bullshit with her. Nobody else did either. Yes, she was *strict*, but she took that word to a place no one else could. She was terrifying.

Addie Metzger. She lived on Meadowbrook Circle. Her husband taught Political Science at AU, in the same department as Ed Williamson, and in fact I later had him—a dry, straightforward man as I recall, and as with the genial Mr. Haggard, I tried to imagine the domestic scene, but came up blank.

I had better luck imagining the scene in the teachers' lounge—Nola and Addie discussing Jimmy Lyle. "He won't be chasing *me* with scissors, I can promise you that, not unless he wants a taste of the cleaver!" And we ain't talking June.

I do recall struggling with multiplication tables (of course I had flash cards), and division in third grade—that may have been when fractions entered the picture too—but I retain little else specific except for a giant toothbrush Mrs.

Metzger kept on top of the lockers, I guess to demonstrate the working parts. And Padge Dorne and his notoriously unsharpened pencils, and Barbara Ball with her plastic case of colored pencils perpetually falling out of her desk (actually, those could be any year), and the only spelling word I ever missed in grammar school: "grey" for "gray." I was only being loyal to my beloved Greyhound Bus Lines—but Mrs. Metzger reacted strictly. It said "gray" in the book—it was Wrong. No argument. Sort of like when she told Mindy it was impolite for girls to perspire.

Like a long ago toothache it is forgotten, but it must have been a trying year. Nose to the grindstone.

Maybe I owe her.

Mrs. Williamson: "Oh yes! I knew her! She was tough—with adults as well as children. I'm sure she was an adequate teacher, but she was an old-fashioned teacher."

I told her we were afraid of her.

"I can understand that."

* * *

Auburn public schools have long been among the best in the state, and when Mrs. Williamson came to Auburn in 1958, she felt it was less of a "hick town" than Montgomery where kids often came shoeless to school, and used "terrible grammar." But at the same time, because of a "wonderful" principal she had had in Montgomery, she felt she was taking a step back. The principal, a woman, ran a tight ship and fostered advanced teaching techniques, such as ability grouping. In Auburn, Mrs. Williamson found a group of teachers who "had been there a hundred years" (I told you they were grandmotherly), and in her view were bogged in outdated methods and, in some cases, competitive self-interest.

The elementary school principal of that era was Mr. Francis Marshall, whose rubber stamp signature I can remember on my report cards. He was a pleasant, friendly man (whose son was later the most marvelous thing a person could be: a drummer in the senior high band)—and what memories I have of him are positive.

Mrs. Williamson had a better seat. "He was always a nice guy." But, she recalled, "the teachers took advantage of him something awful. The person that got the best supplies for her classroom was the person who bothered him the most." She came from a different system of school administration. "I was used to higher standards; everybody was used to Mr. Marshall not taking things too seriously. The teachers did as they pleased. And if he didn't give them what they wanted, they made things miserable for him until he did."

One in particular used to "torture" him. "She was the chairman of them all. In a faculty meeting she did all the talking. I was kind of shocked when I came to Auburn—I didn't know teachers behaved like that."

Which brings me to my fourth grade teacher, Mrs. Hagler.

"Oh Law! She's the one!"

So Hagler was a haggler.

I must hasten to say that I remember Mrs. Hagler as a loveable, good-humored, indulgent lady, and I have only good memories of fourth grade. Well, of course, you say—if she always got her way and got all the best stuff. Looking out for her little scholars, I say. That was the year my three-year-older brother entered the unimaginable territory of junior high with rat paddles, changing classes, personal lockers, and PE. I can remember his classmate Ben Hagler coming by his mother's room to drop off his PE roll every day, and being in some awe of him.

Mrs. Hagler's husband Ben Hagler Sr. had the best garden in Auburn at their house just before the tracks at the intersection of Dean and Opelika Roads, now the site of far less interesting things. Mrs. Hagler had a sense of humor; in my mind's eye she is laughing—also an air of regality; she seemed more to preside than sit. I remember her reading a story to us about some kids who got transported to a Lilliput-type world, retaining only the image of the heroes riding atop a miniature train. I think it was also Mrs. Hagler who read us *Where the Red Fern Grows*. Oh my God—Old Dan and Little Ann—there wasn't a dry eye in the room.

* * *

Meanwhile, on a weedy, wooded lot half a block from my house, they had been building a new elementary school; and just after my tenth birthday I underwent a significant life change and entered fifth grade at brand-new Wrights Mill Road School.

I have mostly fond memories of that year. It was a step up—we were older, more mature, what passed for couples at that tender age began forming, we had parties. The Platter Parade was on WAUD—we also had WJHO in Opelika, and of course BIG BAM in Montgomery—and all it takes is one bar of "Things" or

"Telstar" to take me back to that time. I started wearing glasses for the first time, and I was so self-conscious I hid them at first. The school didn't have the rich layers of distinctive smells and emotions of Samford, but smelled new, with play fields around it—more open than Samford, more modern. Also, as I've bored countless young people by pointing out—no air conditioning. We didn't get that luxury until we entered the brand-new high school in 1966. To my own children, who can't tolerate anything outside of about a 3-degree temperature range in the low/mid-seventies, that's simply inconceivable. They imagine my grade school years as black and white, hot, with pterodactyls circling overhead. The school had no cafeteria either, so we had to bring our own lunches. I had a transportation-themed lunchbox (still have it) and Mama usually had something okay in there, except for sliced boiled egg sandwiches on empty-pantry days. I had never eaten oatmeal cakes before, and was fascinated by the big oval ones Tommy Yeager brought, and before long was demanding them myself. We could buy milk, and this was the era of milk cartons without the gabled roofs, sealed with little strips of aluminum foil, featuring a series of collect-them-all Presidents which set off a collecting frenzy, the rare ultra-modern JFK the most coveted. But the greatest lunches of all time were those of Peter Szilassy. He and his family were refugees from communist Hungary. I had to look up his name to remember how to spell it, and never could pronounce it. Neither could anybody else—to us, he was just Peter See-lushy. He brought exotic cheeses and peppers and sausages. I sat by him and in rapt fascination watched him methodically lay out all that romantic fare. Me with my baloney sandwich. I couldn't match him, but I began putting bell pepper halves on my sandwiches and so forth, and eating them with a good See-lushy-like crunch. Mama didn't make any sandwiches that crunched. We once took a field trip to the Auburn water works, with his mother as a chaperone, driving some big old 50s Pontiac or something. She was a colorful character, whom I liked very much, and I later made some remark referring to her, and her family, as Hungarian. I believe it was actually Mrs. Green who corrected me: "They're not Hungarian, they're *American.*"

Obviously I never forgot that.

If only I could forget how the insufferable jocks from AU who later were our practice teachers/coaches in PE, Bucky Waid for one, tortured unathletic Peter with incredible cruelty. It still makes me sick to think of it.

My fifth grade teacher, you ask. I'm getting to her. I certainly wouldn't leave Mrs. Webster out because she was my favorite of them all, though the one about whom I knew the least—including her first name, which might have been

Lorene or something. Mary Bentley looked up her name in the dictionary and saw that it meant a "weaver." So she became, to us—Weaver. Along with Weblet.

It's not surprising that Mrs. Williamson didn't know Mrs. Webster—in fact, had never heard of her. Neither had we, in 1962—she was new, just moved to Auburn, and carried none of the rap-sheet that attached to all those other hundred-year veterans. She had what Mama always said I had at the beginning of every school year: "a clean slate." She had come from Sylacauga, and I don't think she stayed here too long after us. Except for a small circle of alumni, her name will mean nothing to most people from Auburn if you ask.

She was, I would guess, in her fifties—dignified, plain, with strangely striated teeth, like a dental mishap, and we loved her from the first. I'm not exactly sure why, but looking back I think it may have been because we appreciated not being looked down on, patronized—it was like she saw us not as children but as people—could see in us the adults we would become—and maybe there was something a little sad in that to her. Maybe we responded also to her own humanity—a sense of depth, a web indeed of light and dark. The light predominated—we knew she was good, incapable of being mean or petty or cruel. But the dark was there too. She got terrible migraine headaches, and sometimes laid her head on her desk as we worked on an assignment in total silence. She had a grown daughter—living somewhere else—we never met her. She didn't talk about her much. She lived a few houses down from Mrs. Vowell on Moore's Mill Road, a plain little brick house, sparse and neat inside. We visited her there a few times. Even then, we sensed something melancholy in her. I've assumed all these years it was something gone awry in her previous place, or some feckless man, but Mindy reminded me that she was a widow, that her husband had been killed in a fall at a dam project he was working on. That's sadder somehow than a no-good man. A good man, worthy of her, the last thing between her and loneliness, except for just beginning to mature children. Who knows? Our adoration must have been of some solace to her.

The clearest memory of her I have is of an afternoon when, for some forgotten reason, I had gone to the little breezeway by the principal's office with a top—fifth grade was the height of the top and yo-yo craze—I don't remember and can't imagine the circumstances—but Mrs. Webster came angrily out thinking I had done some wrong which whatever it was I hadn't. Probably framed by somebody. She immediately softened—anger wasn't natural to her, or maybe she was just tired of it, and her flash of it indeed shocked me—but she instantly forgave me and became Weaver again.

She let Sharon Rouse's dog Tony stay in our room sometimes.

I guess she was still up in the other wing, but I really don't remember seeing much of her after that year. Mindy said she returned to Sylacauga after she retired, and remarried. I hope she was happy.

* * *

On to sixth grade—leaving, I think now, my childhood behind and watching the modern world arrive. A lot of things happened that year (1963/4): the advent of Tab, Pommac, zip codes, the Ford Mustang, the Mercury program becoming Gemini, I Have a Dream, the beginnings of Vietnam, Barry Goldwater, Dr. No, twist parties, and above all, the assassination of President Kennedy, and the arrival of the Beatles. And presiding over it all, for us, a quiet, intelligent, unassuming teacher named Mrs. Green.

She lived in a modernistic, vegetation-obscured house at the end of Fontaine Drive—the Greens in their greenery—next door to Jimmy Lyle!—and I knew there was something a little different about her. The words "liberal" and "progressive" weren't in my vocabulary then. I found her husband in the Directory—John C. Green—in the Speech department at the university, I think—and instantly remembered her name when I saw it: Winifred, or Winnie. The memory of her standing, terribly shaken, before the class to tell us President Kennedy had been shot reigns supreme in my memory, but a few other odds and ends have survived.

Rainy days, for one thing—when we couldn't go outside for play period. She'd have us move all the desks and teach us dance steps—"Red River Valley" stands out. We had to act like "gentlemen" and "ladies." Or sing exotic classics: "Aloha Oe" and "Santa Lucia." Maybe she had honeymooned in Hawaii or Italy in some younger brighter world. She also had us write off to foreign countries for tourist information, and I can remember the thrill of receiving those brochures eons later in the mail from the Netherlands, France, Belgium, whatever. I think she was a woman of some culture, and was trying to rub some off on us; trying to let us know that there's more to the world than a small town in Alabama. I remember her primarily standing, holding forth—an imperturbable, decorous, soft spoken woman—the more than meets the eye type. I recall her disquisition one day on the word "literally." She disapproved of its general misuse. No, one didn't "literally" die laughing. Precise but not pedantic, she must have done that with other words and subjects all year, but that's the only one I remember.

She had weekly class officer elections, and Charlie King should have been president-for-life. I have fond memories of Charlie, a good boy, actually doing his long division problems when she left the room, and getting them all right, and fast. She probably had him taking names too. I liked Charlie a lot—it was impossible not to. He grew up to be a veterinarian, and died way too early. I retain a clear image of Cooper King, his father, and his mother—good people. Then there was the day Jon Williams (no relation, but they moved in next door to our old house on Woodfield where his father did experiments on chickens, scandalizing the garbage collectors) puncturing a classroom window with his elbow, spraying the place with blood, and bringing out the frantic side of Winnie. I'm not sure about this, but I bet you they took him to Dr. Thomas. Gentle Ben. The Williams family had a bunch of children, and they called their mother "Ann." I've forgotten when the grading system changed from E, G, S, N, U to A, B, C, D, F, but it had happened by sixth grade, and I recall one report card day when Wells Warren got his and exclaimed, "Straight A's!" I was about as happy for him as a runner-up in Miss America, until I got mine and had straight A's too. I think it was the only time in my public school career.

Mrs. Williamson: "She was a very serious person—very serious about her teaching. She was pretty much a student herself—intellectual. I thought she was bright. She was certainly no Mrs. Umbach."

* * *

These seven women, with whom I spent more face-time than with my own family during the foundation years of my life, were, I know, largely responsible for my view of reality and human behavior. Even later, when we reached rebellious years, it was that invisible solidity we pushed against. There was no escaping it. And look at us today—we didn't succeed.

The reader will notice that these reflections of my early years in Auburn contain few black folks, but that's because I knew few, certainly no peers, in that strictly divided era. I leave off this piece at age twelve, just before all of that was to change. I have long believed that the decency and respect and human values that those early teachers instilled in us in the interest of the status quo had the paradoxical effect of making our generation receptive to the social upheaval of the Civil Rights movement.

The most notable feature of Eudora Welty's famous story "A Worn Path" is the narrative voice, a stand-in for Welty herself traveling the back roads of

Mississippi during the Depression—the consciousness who *saw* Phoenix Jackson, the invisible, because she saw something of her in herself. As I was growing up, just across town a whole class of people lived in another reality that made ours possible but never entered our field of vision. They were invisible. When they came into "our" schools in the eighth grade, we *had* to look. I borrowed one of the most indelible images of my life for my novel *Lake Moon*: Ernest Walker, one of only two or three black people in the school that year, standing by the oak tree on the side of the cafeteria after lunch at Samford School alone and ignored. Not harassed, just ignored. I couldn't fathom an isolation so complete. There was nothing that made the headlines when the schools were racially integrated in Auburn—it happened peacefully. Yes, there are stories we'd rather forget, and we all remember agonizing scenes like mine, but I think the majority of us heard what these no longer invisible people were saying, and knew they were right.

I don't apologize for my memories, or my incurable nostalgia—they are what they are and I'm not going to lie. Yes, we were living in an incredibly privileged bubble, like all privileged bubbles feeding off a vast subscape of injustice below, rendered invisible. I don't feel nostalgia for the injustice but for the innocence. The not knowing. That's why we long for our youth—we crave the sensation of carrying so little past. Even a past with social injustice, doctors in Camel ads, and DDT for lunch.

For anyone interested in the complete history of Auburn, an indispensible book is *Lest We Forget: A History of African Americans of Auburn, Alabama*, compiled by the Committee for the Preservation of Auburn's African-American History. It has many stories to tell. If August Wilson had grown up here, one of his plays would have been set in "The Tasty Shop" in the fifties.

Mrs. Williamson brought a liberal sensibility with her to Auburn in 1958, and except for her church—Holy Trinity Episcopal, fortunately—didn't find many kindred spirits. One she did find was Francis Marshall who she remembers becoming superintendent around 1965, when she was teaching at Dean Road, and knowing her political views, asked her to be his Supervisor of Instruction. She worked the white and black schools, and in the process became one of the first white people ever to enter some of the black schools, where the conditions were deplorable, and she embarked on the exhausting job of furnishing them with equitable supplies and information with relish during that transition era before full integration. They were the most tiring, and most rewarding, years of her working life. At first, when she, a white woman, began making promises, none of the black teachers believed her, but when she delivered, she won their trust. "Oh! You don't know how fun it was to bring things to those teachers. I'd get them to tell me what they needed, and I would arrive with them—things they'd never dreamed of having. It was just a wonderful experience for me. They treated me like I was some sort of white angel. When I left, all the teachers got together and bought me the nicest present."

What about today?

"Oh, it's a different time. The behavior is more complicated now. It's a very different sociological environment. The government got involved—and they don't know anything about education."

Too bad.

"The beginning is so important."

* * *

I remember the little rugs we brought to kindergarten for our naps—I remember having my head down, eyes closed, and thinking, "she" knows somehow that my eyes are closed, that I'm not faking it. Ah, that reassuring belief in an omniscient consciousness above us. And, of course, that's what we've lost in our trek through life—the sense of something above us. Something older, more powerful, wiser. The loneliest movement in life has been the one into that role ourselves.

The past is a blank canvas, our memories the paint. Remembering and creating are the same—moving something from a chamber of our brain into our hands—and not nearly as easy to distinguish as we like to think.

Which is why I don't trust memory.

I know there are bound to be inaccuracies and injustices in these sketches. I'm sorry for that—it hasn't been my intention to offend—but hey, I'm not writing a history article, but a poem. To the Board of Education I would just say, "If you didn't want somebody writing an impressionistic reminiscence fifty years later, why didn't you keep records?"

The silo in Town Creek Park
(formerly Salmon's Pasture)

About the Author

John M. Williams grew up in Auburn and attended Auburn public schools and Auburn University. For five years in the eighties he owned and ran a small printing business, Village Printers. He recently retired from LaGrange College, where he taught for twenty-six years. He was named Georgia Author of the Year for First Novel for his novel *Lake Moon* in 2002. With singer/songwriter Ken Clark he has written five rock'n'roll comedies, with several local productions. With Rheta Grimsley Johnson he co-wrote *Hiram*, a musical play about the early teen years of Hank Williams, recently produced by the Pell City Players in Alabama. He has published a variety of stories, essays, and reviews through the years.

CPSIA information can be obtained
at www.ICGtesting.com
Printed in the USA
FFOW03n1220091216
30192FF